Never the Same

Books by Alexa Bigwarfe

Sunshine After the Storm: A Survival Guide for the Grieving Mother

Lose the Cape: Realities from Busy Modern Moms and Strategies to Surive

Simple and Fun Goal Setting Strategies for Busy Moms! Think like a CEO and Get More Done

Never the Same

Families Forever Changed by Twin to Twin Transfusion Syndrome

Alexa Bigwarfe

Published by Kat Biggie Press
Columbia, SC
info@katbiggiepress.com

Copyright © 2016 Kat Biggie Press

All rights reserved. No part of this publication may be reproduced or transmitted in any form or by any means, including informational storage and retrieval systems, without permission in writing from the copyright holder, except for brief quotations in a review.

ISBN 13: 978-0-9861969-8-0

Library of Congress Control Number: 2016

First Edition: December 2016

10 9 8 7 6 5 4 3 2 1

For Kathryn, always in my heart. We remember all TTTS babies gone too soon.

Contents

INTRODUCTION	9
SINGLE SURVIVORS	19
KATHRYN AND CHARIS	21
CHAYCE AND BRYCE	31
ZACHARY AND ALEX	41
CHASE AND TYLER	47
CAMERON AND COLE	61
MICAH AND SPENCER	75
CREW AND DEX	93
WALKER AND WILLIS	103
DOUBLE SURVIVORS	119
PEYTON AND ADDISON	121
CAMERON AND KATE	133
BENJAMIN AND JD	141
BRADY AND BRENDEN	151
PENN AND CRUZ	163
ELENA AND DIANA	173
LANDON AND LUKE	181

NEVER THE SAME

CHARLIE AND KIERA	193
ADAH AND ABIGAIL	197
GRADY AND HUDSON	203
WILLIAM AND MASON	211
CODY AND CHRISTIAN	217
JORDAN AND ELI	223
EVELYN AND ELIZABETH	227
DOUBLE LOSS	235
JACKALYN AND ALEXA	237
CATHERINE AND HATTIE	249
MATIAS AND MAEL	259
ALANA AND SELENA	265
HEATHERLY ROSE AND WINTER	273
ALLANAH AND LIZ	277
BRAXTON AND CONNOR	283
FOREVER LINKED	291
HERE TO HELP	297
SUPPORTING GRIEVING PARENTS	309
THANK YOU	317

Introduction

I found out early on that I was pregnant with twins. I was just about 6 weeks pregnant, when they saw the two heartbeats. At 8 weeks, the doctor confirmed there were two heart beats and one placenta. Identical twins.

To say I was shocked is an understatement. Each time I returned for a checkup, I expected to see that there was only one heartbeat, but each time, there were two.

For reasons I can't explain, my doctors didn't really talk to me about Twin to Twin Transfusion Syndrome (TTTS). I vaguely remember at the 8-week appointment, the doctor saying nonchalantly something like: "Identical twin pregnancies can be tricky. Sometimes they don't share the placenta evenly, but if that happens, there are things we can do." And that was it.

Until that was *not* it. Again, for reasons I cannot explain, my doctors did not schedule a 16-week ultrasound. I assumed they knew what they were doing, and never questioned it. IF YOU are carrying twins, insist on being regularly monitored.

At the 20-week ultrasound, I waited patiently as the ultrasound tech took her pictures and measurements. Before she finished, she pointed something out to me. "Do you see the black in Baby A's abdomen?" I nodded. "That's fluid. The doctor is going to come in and talk to you now." I immediately started crying. I knew something was wrong. My husband laughed and told me not to jump to conclusions.

I got dressed and went into the room to wait for the doctor. She explained the babies had Twin-to-Twin Transfusion Syndrome (TTTS) and they were Stage 3, meaning one of the babies was already in bad shape. She admitted me to the hospital and transferred me to the care of an Maternal Fetal Medicine OB – or the high risk doctor. Neither my husband nor I knew what was happening, but we thought we were losing both babies that day.

Our story is only one of many, many stories about TTTS. I share the full story in Chapter one of the book, but I wanted to give a brief introduction on how this book came to be. After our twins were born, I started blogging to bring awareness to TTTS. I began a series on my blog TTTS Tuesday, and asked other parents to share their stories. Many of the stories in this book were first featured there. The outcomes are different, the stories are different, but the underlying theme is the same. TTTS is a very unpredictable and dangerous condition, and should be considered critical from the start. There are still so many medical providers who do not recognize the severity of this disease, and so many who do not fully understand the treatments, the courses of action, and the complications that can occur from this disease.

What is TTTS?

TTTS affects identical twins who share a placenta.

Fun fact - did you know that ANYONE can become pregnant with identical twins? I always thought they were hereditary, but that's fraternal twins. The medical field still does not know what causes an egg to split, but that is what results in identical twins. One egg that splits into two (or more!) identical fetuses. And that can happen to anyone.

Because the babies share a placenta, the blood supplies can become connected resulting in shared blood circulation.

This connection allows blood to pass from one twin to another, and with TTTS, the blood is not transferred proportionately

The "donor" twin winds up transferring blood to the "recipient" twin, reducing the blood flow to the donor, slowing their growth and reducing their amniotic fluid levels

The "recipient" receives too much blood flow, which can cause polyhdramnios - or too much fluid, and can lead to heart failure and hydrops, along with other complications

When TTTS develops prior to 26 weeks, it often results in death of one or both babies, or severe disabilities

If you are pregnant with identical twins, or know someone who is, please seek out as much information as you can. And if you do not feel comfortable with the information you are receiving from your OB, FIND A NEW DOCTOR.

The TTTS Foundation can help you find a specialist in your area.

Are there warning signs?

YES.

Warning signs of TTTS in the mother include: rapid growth of the womb, a uterus that measures large for dates, abdominal pain, tightness or uterine contractions, sudden increases in body weight, and swelling of hands and feet.

Over the past few years I have connected with so many parents who have fought the battle with TTTS. We all have different stories and different outcomes. Some have two (or more!) survivors, some have no survivors, some have survivors and angels... but sadly, there is one thing that I find many - not all, but many of us have in common.

Our doctors were not informed.

Or if they were informed, they chose not to do any new research or offer all options to the patient. And in some cases, somebody just plain and simple <u>dropped the ball</u>. For example, in my case, we rotate through the doctors in the practice. I saw a different doctor almost each appointment. And I think in my case, that was not good. One of the doctors told me after the fact that "she did not know why they did not do an ultrasound at 16 weeks" because they normally do with twins.

Sigh. Big sigh.

It is frustrating to hear these stories. And it makes me angry.

But I can do something about it. It's called awareness and education.

Are there Treatment Options

Yes.
- Fetoscopic laser photocoagulation of chorionic plate vessels – or Placental laser surgery. This is done to destroy the connecting vessels. Pioneered in 1988 by Dr. Julian De Lia at the University of Utah, the operation is the only treatment that can disconnect the twins' shared circulations to stop the transfusion of blood.
- Reduction Amniocentis, or Amnio Reductions. This is the most common procedure and is the draining of extra fluid from the sac of the recipient twin. Amnio reduction can help provide more room for the donor baby. It is usually performed multiple times in the pregnancy.
- Selective reduction or termination of pregnancy, depending on the severity of the situation

TTTS Kills a LOT of Babies

It shocks most people when they hear that TTTS

results in the loss of more babies than SIDS each year, but it's the sad truth. The Centers for Disease Control and Prevention (CDC) estimate approximately 2000 babies pass away from SIDS each year. Yet more than 5600 babies are diagnosed with TTTS annually, resulting in the death of 80-100% that do not receive some sort of treatment, and losses as high as 50% in babies that do receive treatment. This dat comes from the USA National Center for Health Statistics. And this doesn't even take into consideration the fact that spontaneous pregnancy loss and pregnancy terminations that occur prior to 20 weeks go uncounted by the C.D.C.. So the TTTS cases are most likely much higher.

The difference seems to be that EVERY baby can be affected by SIDS, whereas TTTS only affects identical twins. However, since anyone is capable of having identical twins (they do not know why the egg splits), it is no less important to recognize the severity of TTTS and to educate OB/GYNs and fetal specialists. We hope that awareness efforts will lead to TTTS being recognized as such a significant risk, and that more babies will be saved.

This book is not intended to be any type of medical guide. Rather, we've collected the stories of parents and families who have been through TTTS. We want the world to realize that, whether a family loses 1, both, or neither of their babies, this horrible syndrome changes all of us forever. You'll see as you read the stories that all of us have fought significant challenges. Most of the babies with TTTS are born very preterm. You'll read a lot of stories of time spent in the Neonatal Intensive Care Unit (NICU), and about the many challenges that arise when babies are born so early.

Some of the problems TTTS babies face include:
- Problems related to prematurity
- Anemia
- Polycythemia
- Hydrops fetalis
- Heart disease
- And more

Our goal of this book is to spread more awareness, but it is also an outlet for families to share their stories, celebrate their babies, and remember the many who did not survive. If you're reading this book, you've either gone through TTTS, been recently diagnosed, or are a family or friend of someone who has. We hope our stories will create more understanding, and help all of us. As you read the stories shared in this book, you will see that regardless of the outcome, none of us will ever be the same.

TTTS changed all our lives forever.

Part 1
Single Survivors

Single Survivors

I chose to start the book with stories of single survivors. Partly out of selfish reasons because my TTTS pregnancy ended with only one survivor.

There's really no perfect way to organize the book, but I found that outcome seemed a logical way to keep the stories together. So we start with single survivors.

Over the last five years I have become personal friends with so many other TTTS families. As I compiled the book and re-read the recollections from the mothers and fathers, of what is truly a nightmare situation, my heart once again recognized what a lousy card we were all dealt with TTTS.

*Kathryn and Charis
Chayce and *Bryce
Zachary and *Alex
Chase and *Tyler
Cameron and *Cole
Crew and *Dex
Walker and *Willis
*Denotes the "angel" twin

Kathryn and Charis

My daughters were monochorionic-diamniotic (Mo/Di) twins - one placenta, two sacs. Twin to Twin Transfusion Syndrome (TTTS) occurs in roughly 15-20% of Mo/Di twins, and sadly is the cause of more deaths of babies each year than SIDS, yet it is still relatively unknown and often not treated when and how it should be.

We were officially diagnosed with TTTS at 20W and 2 days during our regularly scheduled Anatomy ultrasound (U/S). My doctor's notes from that day state:

"Anatomy u/s today reveals TTTS. One fetus with poly/90% pericardial effusion/ascites. Other baby with oligo/10%. Discordance 46%. Will need to transfer to MFM." Translated that means - one baby has way too much fluid at 90% and the other has 10% and there is a 46% difference in their sizes."

Baby A (Kathryn) was 50% too large at the time and

Baby B was 50% too small. Their weight differences were 100% (16 oz and 8 oz.).

Sadly, as I begged my OB to tell me what we could do, she doctor told me "nothing could be done" to save them. And then she admitted me into the hospital. That day as they wheeled me to Labor and Delivery, I thought I was losing both of my babies. I am sure half of the hospital heard me wailing and sobbing as the Medical Tech wheeled me across the hospital.

Thankfully, that doctor was wrong. And since then I have come to realize that many OB/GYNs know very little about TTTS and because of this lack of knowledge, babies are lost.

September 28, 2011, I was hospitalized immediately. The next morning the Maternal Fetal Manager (MFM or high risk OB/GYN) visited me and began to tell me about our options.

We could do nothing, and both babies would die.

We could proceed with an amnio reduction (reduction of the fluids in the amniotic sac to try and return the babies to a normal balance) which could produce preterm labor. At only 20 weeks, there would be few options to save the babies.

Or, he mentioned, there is an option of laser surgery. Fetal laser ablation, in which they would sever some of the connected vessels. However, the doctor told that because I had an anterior placenta (on the front of my abdomen in front of my belly button), we were ineligible for the laser surgery. (As you read through other stories, you'll find he was wrong.)

This left is really with only one option - amnio reduction.

So on Thursday September 29, 2011 we had our first amnio reduction at 20w3d. It was amazing to watch. It was somewhat uncomfortable to have the large needle inserted into my abdomen, but it was cool to watch the babies. For almost an hour they withdrew fluids out of Kathryn's sac. Kathryn tried several times to grab the tip of the needle. It was cute. Yes, that seems really strange as I reread this story that I would describe that as "cute". But when you think you might be watching the last activities of your precious babies, every moment matters. A whopping 500 ML of fluid was removed from Kathryn's side of the sac. That's an IMPRESSIVE amount of fluid.

I was monitored all day for signs of preterm labor. Once it appeared that we were in the clear, I could go home to my other two children.

Over the next several weeks we held our breath as we waited for time to pass. The doctors told us we had to make it to 24 weeks to even be considered viable, and at that point, that needed to be our main goal. I went on bedrest (as much as a woman with a four-year-old and an 18-month-old can be!) and we visited the doctors every week for ultrasounds. Amazingly, the babies stayed stable. Kathryn's hydrops (fluid building up around two or more bodily cavities) did not go away, but it remained stable. Baby B was growing very slowly but she continued to grow, her bladder continued to be visible, and although she was "shrink wrapped" in the membrane separating the babies, she was not "stuck". Her fluids stayed right around 2-3 CM, which was an acceptable amount and allowed her to continue to get nourishment, albeit very little.

At 24 weeks, we took a turn for the worse. Kathryn's heart was worsening... the tricuspid valve was no longer functioning, and the fluid continued to build tremendously. Her abdomen, at 24 weeks, measured the size of a baby at 32 weeks gestation! Baby B, Charis, was still too tiny to be viable.

This was a scary day as we weighed our options. We were once again admitted to the hospital, and this time, since we were at the 24-week point, I was put on magnesium sulfate (AWFUL!!!!) and given steroid shots to help prepare their lungs.

Let me just do a short interlude on mag. Many women who are at risk of preterm delivery wind up taking this. It makes you HOT and ornery! I wanted to vomit, I wanted to scream, I wanted to hurt the nurse. Mothers of twins with TTTS are often in for a rough ride. So if you know someone going through it right now, be kind to her. She's miserable.

Three days later, on 10/27 (24 w and 3 Days) we had our 2nd amnio reduction as well as a paracentesis... this time they also stuck a needle into Kathryn's abdomen and withdrew over 200 ML of fluid out of her belly. Again, we worried about pre-term labor, especially since this procedure could really cause Kathryn distress. By introducing a needle into Kathryn's abdomen, there was a risk of destabilizing her. The little baby (Charis) still had a 0% of survival if we were to go into labor at this point, (she was only measuring at 22 weeks) so we waited with great anticipation to see if the procedure would cause premature labor. Thankfully the babies tolerated it well, and I could go home that evening.

The following week showed no improvement. Kathryn continued to take on fluids and the little baby was growing very slowly. At our appointment on 11/1 the doctor's notes stated: "Baby A has 6.6 Fluid, Baby B had 2.0"; the comment was made that "Twin A has worsening hydrops". It didn't look good. All of us cried (the nurse, the u/s tech, me) as the doctor began to offer us other options.

We once again discussed our options. Now we were given the option of going to the Children's Hospital of Philadelphia (CHOP) to have a tubal ligation - a procedure that would terminate Kathryn. At this point she had such a small chance of survival and keeping her alive was threatening the chances for Charis's survival. Charis was still so small, and growing so very slowly. If Kathryn's condition triggered labor, neither baby would survive.

We said no. I was not going to give up on Kathryn, and besides, there were no guarantees baby B would survive either once her sister was terminated.

On 11/8 baby B's fluid levels dropped to 1.2 CM. Not good. The intertwin discordance was 70.5%; but worse, reverse end diastolic flow (REDF) was identified. Briefly, she was starting to return fluids back (reverse flow) and this was very bad. We were once again admitted to hospital - and this time we believed delivery was imminent.

However, the babies had other plans in mind. Over the next 32 days, I remained hospitalized on fluids and oxygen, and tons of protein. (As a side note, research has shown that side lying bedrest, on the left side, combined with a steady intake of protein throughout the day – sipping on Boost all day – has made a huge difference for fetuses with TTTS.) If the babies continued to stay stable, we were just going to leave well enough alone. We did have *weekly* amnio reductions, (can I just tell you how horrific that needle is and what an uncomfortable procedure this was to endure??) and another paracentesis (aspirations of ascites) to draw fluids from Kathryn. Our hope was that withdrawing more fluids would allow her lungs space to grow.

The doctors didn't really like to talk percentages with me when it came to survival. And when they stopped talking about other options of treatment for Kathryn (at one point they were considering a transfer to Medical University of South Carolina so that she could have surgery on her heart after birth), I knew that they had little hope for her.

After we got to about 28 weeks and Charis was finally over 500 grams, the doctor finally started saying he thought she would now have about an 80% chance of survival. He never talked about Kathryn anymore.

On 12/10 (30 W and 5 days) I began having large contractions and went into labor. In the best interest of the babies, I had an emergency cesarean following the diagnosis of preeclampsia and non-reassuring fetal heart rate testing. (My greatest concern was that I'd been on blood thinners while ins the hospital, and had just received a shot of heparin that morning!)

Charis (Baby B) was actually born first, and from

then on became baby A. She weighed 1lb 10 oz. but initially breathed on her own and even cried at delivery. It was the sweetest little sound – like a bird chirping!

Kathryn weighed 4lb 5 oz. (largely due to excess fluids), and was not breathing. Because Kathryn's swollen belly took up so much room, her lungs were too small for her body, and she had to be resuscitated and intubated. They immediately withdrew an insane amount of fluid from her little abdomen, that was severely distended.

Although they stabilized her for the next 24 hours, they were unable to stop the fluid from continuing to build up, and her arterial blood pressure remained too low. Despite a good fight, Kathryn died on day 2 of life (after 52 hours) "with complications of respiratory distress and congenital heart disease". Her death certificate however directly states cause of death as "hydrops fetalis."

Tiny spent 84 days in the NICU. These were long and tiresome days and nights. She had multiple blood transfusions, a couple of really scary nights, and eventually had to have a g-tube surgically placed because she could not suck, swallow, and breathe at the same time. We took her home without a monitor, but with a feeding tube, that miraculously only had to stay in a little over 3 months.

In the following weeks, months, and for the first year of her life, our schedule was full of appointments, therapy, surgery follow ups. But she is a true miracle. At the time of this publication, Tiny is five years old, completely caught up, and has no residual health concerns.

We are so grateful for her but we still miss her sister every day.

Chayce and Bryce

Jennifer Scott

Of all the parents I have met through TTTS, Jennifer is one that I share one of the closest bonds. She was there for me from the very beginning to provide encouragement and support. We laughed over things that only parents who have had one twin die from TTTS could laugh about. We've helped other mamas together, we've supported each other, and we've shared this journey of grief and healing.

Chayce and Bryce

In March 2010, after two early unexplainable miscarriage's, we found out we were pregnant with identical twins!

Surprise!

We were so happy and scared at the same time. The

first part of the pregnancy was good, besides my uncontrollable all day sickness! We got to watch our two very active playful, babies play together on our monthly ultrasounds. Little did we know how wonderfully important these moments were. We have an ultrasound picture of Bryce grabbing Chayce's face and kissing his forehead.

On July 21,2010, we found out we were having boys. The same day we found out my sweet boys, Bryce and Chayce had twin-to-twin transfusion syndrome. I just remember my OB/GYN, who was not only my Dr. But my friend and one of my greatest allies in this battle, holding me as we cried together.

We were sent to Cincinnati children's hospital, where they knew a little bit more about this horrible syndrome. During the following weeks, we went back and forth (we live in Louisville, KY) to Cincinnati numerous times. After, millions of tests, scans, and meetings and about two weeks it was decided we would undergo an amino-reduction (drain some of the amniotic fluid) to relieve some of the pressure off of Bryce's side and give Chayce some more room.

Bryce the bigger of the two (our little recipient) showed no signs of heart damage, or hydrops, as we were told that this was the biggest risk to him. They then explained to us Chayce our little tiny fella (donor) already showed dilated ventricles in his brain, from his lack of nutrients, and he was "stuck," shrink wrapped by the very membrane that was supposed to be protecting him.

The doctors told us he was in the most danger of the two, now. After the reduction and a couple more trips back and forth to Cincy, our boys' fluid levels were staying stable and their health and growth was beginning to improve, I began to let my guard down and finally think, "wow I can breathe."

Then on Friday August 6, 2010 we were told there had been a sudden spike in Bryce's fluid again and a drop in Chayce's, he had become "stuck" again. Both boys remained stable with no new health concerns but it was now time to consider surgery. Chayce had a very little chance of survival even with surgery, but a 0% chance without it. Bryce's only threat at that time was Chayce, if we did not have the surgery and Chayce were to pass away, it would cause all the blood to rush to Bryce and could cause a stroke, death, or severe neurological damage. So, surgery was the only choice to give both of our beautiful boys a fighting chance.

On the morning of Monday August 9, 2010, we underwent the Placental ablation surgery, as this was my boy's last chance of survival. After the surgery was over, the doctors cheered and exclaimed this was a fantastic success, they had completed the "perfect split" and Chayce (Donor)was now receiving 60% while Bryce (recipient) was receiving 40%, both boys were alive and looking great!

The next morning on August 10, 2010 with great excitement from the ultrasound tech, we had an ultrasound to see our boys. We began with Chayce, our little fragile donor. He had pulled through and he was moving all around!

Then next to our sweet baby Bryce or big strong recipient. He just laid there asleep with his thumb in his mouth. Or Sweet, brave strong Boy had gone to Heaven to live with God and watch over his twin brother forever.

The doctors were all in shock; they could not believe Bryce has been the one to pass. They couldn't explain it. We were told to go home, be with family, rest and come back in 1 week.

One week later we went back for our follow up and we were told that even though Chayce had survived the surgery and the first week after, we needed to prepare ourselves for the near future, Chayce wouldn't survive this, and we needed to plan a funeral for both of our boys. We were told all these statistics, and warned of infections. They told us how we were only at 24 weeks, how soon my body would go into labor, and he more than likely would be born in the next couple of weeks and that Chayce was to weak and could not survive. We were told that even if we could hold off labor until he was viable, and/or by some miracle he was to survive, he would have gross neurological deficits, developmental delays and he would never walk, talk, or breath on his own.

We came home to Louisville and I just lost it. How was I supposed to do this? How could I continue to fight as hard as I could for Chayce, while my heart ached so badly for Bryce?!?! I felt like a horrible, broken mommy, my heart was shattered and torn, I felt like it was going to explode. I was holding onto hope fighting for one, while completely devastated mourning the other. So I went to see my Dr., back in Louisville, and she rushed into the room and hugged me as we cried together and she told me that as always, she would continue to fight right alongside of us and that she had faith that Chayce could and would make it! Also, she let me know it was ok to be sad and cry for Bryce. I am beyond lucky to have such a wonderful, caring soul, in my life, let alone as my dr. I can never in this lifetime express my gratitude to this beautiful woman and friend, i truly believe with my all my heart, we would not have made it, and we would not be where we are physically, mentally, or emotionally without her.

NEVER THE SAME

No matter how heartbroken and scared I was, I just refused to accept that Chayce couldn't make it, he had fought so hard, and was so brave and strong! He was/is my child and I would not/ will not give up on him! I trust that the doctors. I know they must go by their statistics and what they have seen. But I had hope, I believe in miracles and I had faith in my child and in God.

So, we hoped and prayed for my little bitty boy to hold on and cook a little longer and to pull through. He had his big strong guardian angel, my sweet brave Bryce to watch over him and hold his hand. Well over the next 10 weeks, I was seen twice a week to monitor Chayce's growth which was slow but steady, also I was given two rounds of steroids to help his lungs grow at 33 weeks and then on November 11, the ultrasound showed he had not grown any in the past two weeks and had fallen off the percentile.

The doctors decided to admit me and monitor him until the following morning, giving my parents and brothers time to get here from Texas. On November 12, 2010, Bryce Lee Scott (born asleep) at a little under a pound and Chayce Allen Scott, 3lbs 5oz. and 17 inches long were born at 34 weeks! Chayce had not only made it, but he scored all 9s and 10s on the agar scale and was breathing on his own!

We stayed in the NICU 21 days, and the day we left, the funeral home called us to let us know we could come pick up Bryce's ashes (he had been cremated). We finally got to bring both our boys home. Not the way we had dreamed, not in two car seats, not in matching outfits, but together.

As for Chayce, we have small struggles, we have had many hospital stays, tests, procedures, surgeries, doctors, therapists and specialist appointments. but he amazes me every day! He is a true miracle. Every day I think of the son and brother we have lost and thank god for the one we have! I am so proud both of my boys they both fought so hard and Chayce continues every day! They said my son would never live, he did, they told me Chayce wouldn't breathe on his own, he did, they told me he would never walk, talk on his own, he had to chance of living a "normal" life, he lives an extraordinary life!! He is a happy healthy 4-year-old little boy, who developmentally is right on track, even ahead in some areas, developmentally he has no deficits! He of course will always have health issues, specialists, and physical therapy but, He shows me and all his doctors that he is a fighter and is going to be just fine! He has had a very long hard road but he has a sweet little angel by his side to help him along the way. I am so very honored to be their mommy.

In 2012 we decided to have another baby. It was the scariest, most healing experience of my life this far. While it was a "standard" pregnancy, I was scared, all the time, I was more than aware of all the things that could go wrong, I was constantly waiting for "the bad news", but with every good appointment, every heartbeat heard, movement felt, with every week passed, I took a deep breath and began to enjoy the good. I really began to enjoy and take in every moment of being pregnant. I realized all I knew was "bad" or "not ok", and that I needed this beautiful healthy girl growing in my belly as much, if not more than she needed me. I realized I hated myself for "letting" this horrible thing (TTTS) happen to my boys, to my family. I hated my body, it had failed me, more importantly it failed my boys. As this beautiful girl grew and thrived, she helped me to forgive myself, to truly realize it wasn't my fault, and I started to "forgive" my body.

I delivered our beautiful daughter Mckynzie Margaret Scott on July 12, 2013 at 39 weeks!!! She was 8lbs 9oz and 21 in. long. After she was born, I heard her cry and then they laid her on my chest. I got to hold her, nurse her... I got to keep my baby right there, with me. She roomed in with me. I changed her diapers, held her when she cried, nursed her when she was hungry, I got to take care of my baby.

I don't think people realize how important that is for a mother and father to be able to have their healthy baby, "room in" and be a mommy and daddy. NOT have to go "visit" your baby in the NICU, ask to touch your baby, or have to schedule when to hold him or her. The appreciation was not lost on me.

TTTS robbed me of not only Bryce, but of the whole pregnancy, birth and newborn experience. It was extremely healing to be able to experience that "normal" birth and newborn experience.

I will never be "healed", and i will never stop morning the loss of not only Bryce, but all that comes with the loss of a child, the loss of a "normal" pregnancy and the loss of myself. I will never be the carefree, no worries girl I was before, I will never know a sense of naive, during easy carefree pregnancy. It has taken a long time, but I have found my peace. Thankfully I have such a wonderful, supportive family, and group of friends. I have found of some my dearest friend through this journey and I am so very thankful for them. I have found my new normal, which includes missing my baby, being a "worrier" and accepting that I'll never be "back" to who I was before.

I've found little pieces of my old self and then there are the pieces I'll never get back, and that is ok. I have had to learn to love the new me, and my new normal.

Zachary and Alex

Wen Smith

I met Wendy through the TTTS Grief Support Group, or maybe it was the Survivors with Guardian Angels. Either way, we both lost one twin and got to take one twin home. Wendy has taken her story and written a book - called "Toughest Teeniest Twin Soldiers.

Zachary and Alex from "Toughest Teeniest Twin Soldiers"

Three years ago began the shock of our lives with the news: we're carrying identical twins! Less than a month later, we were diagnosed with Twin to Twin Transfusion Syndrome. It was St Patrick's Day when our perinatal specialist decided to refer us to U.S.C. for intervention because he felt our case of TTTS was severe enough for laser surgery. I can remember sitting there in the lobby nervously playing with my green jewelry; consumed by such an intense fear of the unknown. My back ached so badly and I was so scared. As the doctor spoke with us, tears streamed down my cheeks. The thought of traveling out of town to try and save our unborn babies terrified me. The thought of losing these babies terrified me even more.

On March 22nd, we met Dr. Chmait and his amazing team for the first time. And although we did have TTTS, it was not severe enough to risk the surgery. (Incidentally, our twin niece and nephew were born this very day: Maddison and Mitchell.) Now, fast forward a week later and we're back at Dr. Chmait's. Our TTTS has gotten much worse. Baby Alex is critical and Baby Zachary is "stuck" with no visible bladder.

Although we underwent laser surgery to save our boys (this was on April Fool's Day, 2010, and was the most amazing experience of my lifetime [aside from giving birth]); sadly, Baby A (Alex) passed away three weeks later due to heart failure. This is a moment I will never forget. No person should ever have to experience that shock and anguish. Alexander will always be our little angel. April 21, 2010 will always be remembered as "Alex's Angelversary". I carried the twins for five more weeks before preterm labor awakened me on the morning of May 28th, 2010. I drove myself to the hospital, and our twins were delivered emergently at 28 weeks. One fighter was born into the NICU (Zachary Alexander) and his angel twin rose to Heaven. And our lives will never be the same...

In 2011, I published a short book, "Toughest Teeniest Twin Soldiers: Living and Dying Through TTTS" because I really felt compelled to tell our story.

Furthermore, it has become very important to me to reach out to other families so they know they are not alone. Today I also feel very fortunate to work in healthcare where I have the opportunity to reach out to others, including medical professionals as well as various families who may not have even heard of TTTS. I proudly wear my TTTS swag and talk about it whenever I can. I love it when people ask me to talk about it. It used to feel strange, but now, I feel proud! I'm proud of my survivor and I'm proud of the friends I've made since our lives have been touched by TTTS. And I'm even proud to say that I have a precious angel twin. This angel has even graced me with visits on two occasions when I've hit my rock bottom.

Which leads me to my next point: I'm not going to act like I don't feel emotional and ripped off when I see twins. It reminds me of what I was "supposed to have". And sometimes I find myself extremely annoyed by twins in matching outfits (what's up with that anyway;

please enlighten me?)! But more than anything, I am feeling blessed. Because Zachary was the twin nobody expected to survive. And look at him today: he's thriving! His charming personality earned him the nickname "The Mayor of Las Vegas" at a very young age! Even as a teeny infant with oxygen tubing in his nose, his smile and laughter were contagious. So, this is what we celebrate today. We know his brother is still with us. That box on the shelf with his ashes is just a memorial. And someday, we'll all be together again. Meanwhile, we're singing and dancing and playing and loving and laughing our way through lives.

In fact, I participate in a bereavement support group for baby loss families called "Healing Hearts Giving Hope". One of the moms shared this beautiful reality: Someone asked her if she'd do it all over again, and even though it caused her excruciating pain, the baby she lost also brought her intense joy!! She would never forget how active he was in the womb and what a show off he was during all the ultrasounds. She experienced awful guilt thinking maybe she could have prevented his death, but now, years later, she is at peace. He is part of her family. Wow! And another mom had her son's NICU bracelet tattooed to her wrist in white ink. So much raw and heart-wrenching beauty and I'm so grateful I have such a network of amazing families to share this with. I could go on and on, but for now, that is all…

With hugs and kisses from our twins to yours!! ~Wen

Chase and Tyler

Christina Sporer

Chase and Tyler's story

I found out I was pregnant the week after July 4th 2010. It was my first pregnancy and just like all first-time parents, my husband Jason and I were both nervous and excited.

A few weeks later I experienced some spotting and I nervously called my GYN office. The doctor told us to come in right away for an ultrasound. I remember holding Jason's hand on the way into the office and telling him, "I can't lose this baby."

Twenty minutes later I found myself laying on the examination table for an internal ultrasound. The doctor looked at the screen and said words that no woman in that position wants to hear..."Hmm, this is interesting!" "What's interesting?" I slowly asked.

"This is one fertilized egg, this is a sack, and this is

another fertilized egg." After a few moments of stunned silence, I said "Twins?" My husband got up from his chair in the corner of the room and peered nervously at the screen. "Are there any more in there?" he asked.

We laughed and she assured us that it was just the two of them and that it was too soon to tell if they were identical.

My husband and I walked back to the car in stunned silence that slowly turned into excitement. Jason was especially excited as he is an identical twin.

The first person I called was my friend Kristi. She had two miscarriages and I called her as soon as I started spotting. She had been praying for me all morning.

"I have good news and interesting news." I told her. "What's going on?" she asked. I could hear the apprehension in her voice. "They're both fine!" "No way," she replied. She sounded as stunned as I had been just a few minutes earlier. This was the first of many such fun phone calls and encounters we would have that day.

We got to tell our families, our friends, and our co-workers. My boss was so excited after she saw the ultrasound that she announced it over our building loud speaker.

Like most pregnant women, I also made the

announcement on Facebook and followed up with new posts after every ultrasound.

At 14 weeks, we found out that our twins were identical. I posted about this on Facebook and soon I received a private message from an old college friend.

Her name was Tova Gold. I had gone to college with her and hung out with her often. We had not kept in very close touch over the years and months later she told me how nervous she was to write me this message.

You see she knew I would not want to hear what she had to say. No one wants to hear what she has to say because no one wants to believe that babies die. Yet she took a risk and shared the story of her daughters who are forever nicknamed Sunshine and Daisy.

Sunshine and Daisy were also identical twins. This means that like my boys they came from one egg that split (mono chorionic), lived together in one sack, and shared the same placenta. This is the most dangerous kind of twin because it means they are at risk for Twin to Twin Transfusion, a disease that is caused by an imbalance of the way the babies receive food and nutrients from the placenta. Sunshine and Daisy had succumbed to this disease in 2009.

She assured me that this disease does not happen to all twin pregnancy's and that she didn't want me to be upset, she wanted me to be informed so that I could be proactive about this disease and the pregnancy.

She sent me the link to her blog and also the link to the Twin to Twin Transfusion Foundation web site. I began to research the disease so I could become informed in case the worst happened.

I continued to research the disease and I found out that signs of TTTS could pop up around 16 weeks. Before our 16-week appointment I sent out an e-mail to all of my friends and family to please pray that we would not get bad news at our ultrasound.

I was so nervous on the way to the doctors that day. I received a text from my friend Kelly that read "don't be nervous, I just know you will find out that they are two healthy girls."

She was half right. That day we found out we were having two healthy, identical twin boys. Another set of Sporer twins to rival my husband and his brother. Both boys looked healthy and seemed to be growing as they should.

Now that we knew the sex we could start to have fun. We went to Babies R Us to register and picked tons of cute matching outfits for our boys. Two of everything. Two cribs, two high chairs, two teddy bears....

Then came our week 18 Perinatologist visit. The usual routine was that the ultrasound tech would scan the twins and print the pictures. At the same time the pictures were able to be viewed in the Perinatologist's private office. Most times the tech would just show him a few of the pictures after we were done. Some days he would come in for a short consultation but other times we would not see him at all.

The scan of baby A seemed to be fine. We got a lot of good shots. He was being still and behaving. Baby B looked like a crazy person. He would not sit still! We joked that he would become our problem child.

Now the scan was done and Jason wanted to go get the car while I saw the doctor and got dressed. This was our normal routine but today the tech asked him to wait. She also asked the student technician to wait up. The two technicians went out into the hall and then Jason and I waited for them to return. My anxiety was mounting as the minutes ticked by. I looked at him and said "Something's wrong." He tried to reassure me but I could tell that he felt it too.

Finally, the Perinatologist came back and uttered the words that we had been afraid to hear. It was stage 1 Twin to Twin Transfusion. Baby A was so still because he was saran wrapped in my uterus with 1.5 cm's of fluid. Baby B was so wild because he was overrun with 8.5 cm's of fluid at the largest visible pocket.

The doctor told us that he was going to make us an appointment at C.H.O.P (Children's Hospital of

Philadelphia) for that coming Thursday but in the meantime, he would like to perform an amniotic fluid reduction on Baby B that would hopefully stabilize the T.T.T.S.

Jason held my hand as I lay on the table surrounded by Dr. Aroldi and several of his assistants. I couldn't look at the screen or the needle so we changed the subject at talked about our favorite vacation destinations. I also spent a lot of time praying.

When he was finished, I remember the Doctor said that Baby A, the "stuck" baby gave a little kick. He took this as a sign of hope that he would be okay.

We went home from the hospital and began to call our friends to deliver the sad news. I remember lying on the couch and sobbing uncontrollably.

The next day I called Tova and we had a long conversation about T.T.T.S and the many options that might lie ahead. I was so grateful to have her to talk to.

Finally, it was Thursday and time to get up at the crack of dawn to drive to Philadelphia. We had a day long appointment at C.H.O.P.

The synopsis of the day was that both boys were alive and seemed small but healthy. They had reached stage 1 TTTS but they were not candidates for surgery at this time because the amnio-reduction worked and fluids remained balanced. If the fluids became unbalanced throughout the pregnancy, we would re-visit the option of surgery.

The recommendation was made that we have 2 ultrasounds per week to monitor the twins.

We walked out into the night sky feeling hopeful about our situation. I told Jason I would like to name them. I called Baby A Chase. This is the name that I picked. I wanted to name the weaker twin. Every time I thought of him giving his little kick after the amnio I would start to cry. I worried that I would never get to hold him in this lifetime and I wanted to give him the one thing that I could- a name. Baby B was called Tyler. I figured that he would be with us and it would be nice to let Jason name his surviving son.

As the weeks rolled on we became increasingly hopeful that all of us would come through this pregnancy alive. The ultrasounds all went well, fluids remained stable and both fetuses continued to look small but strong.

At our 31-week ultrasound Dr. Aroldi told us that he was very pleased with the results and was looking forward to watching us raise two healthy twin boys.

At this point I started to let down my guard. I believed that we were out of the woods. That T.T.T.S was a nightmare that occurred in the beginning of my pregnancy but would almost be forgotten by the end.

We went back to behaving like "normal" first time parents. We took a tour of the hospital, began to plan the nursery, and I even bought a set of new matching stockings for our whole family.

Then came the second week in December 2010. It has been almost two years now but my memory of that week has not faded. Monday December 13th, I went to the chiropractor. Something didn't feel "right" after that visit. I'm in no way saying that the chiropractor caused Tyler's demise, I just think that he died right around the time of that visit. There was no pain but I felt like something was wrong.

The next day was my hair appointment. The woman who cut my hair was a relative of my friend Shirley. We had a nice conversation about my twins but in the back of my head I heard this voice that kept saying to me "He's already gone." I dismissed the premonition and chalked it up to nerves.

I woke up on Wednesday December 15th and prepared to go to my Perinatologist appointment. Ever since we found out about the T.T.T.S we always made sure that I wasn't alone for my appointments. If Jason had to work I would bring my mother or a friend

Jason did not have to work that day but he had been out late with his friends. I felt like something was wrong and I begged him to come with me but he refused. He told me I was over-reacting and I would be fine.

Something did not sit right with me. I knew I shouldn't be alone but by this time it was too late to find someone to go with me so I got in my car and drove to the doctor's office.

Twenty minutes later I was laying on the table as my favorite ultrasound tech Jennifer (the one who had assisted during my amnio reduction) rubbed warm jell over my tummy. The scan of Chase went well and then she moved on to Tyler. She rubbed the wand over my belly for several seconds before she exclaimed "I can't find a heartbeat" and laid her head down on my stomach.

Tyler

It wasn't a complete shock. "Does this happen often?" I asked her, and she shook her head no. I asked her what would happen now and she told me she had to go get the Perinatologist.

Dr. Bell was on duty that day. He entered the room after a few minutes and offered me his apologies. He looked at Tyler and then did a checkup of Chase who seemed to be doing okay.

He told me that he thought I would have to deliver that day. "At 26 weeks?" I whispered. "He won't be the smallest one in there."

I got dressed and Jen walked me to the hospital, which was attached to the Doctor's office. We had to go to C3 which was the third floor of the Centennial Wing, the high-risk pregnancy floor.

Jennifer introduced me to the RN on duty, Shelly, and she walked me into a large empty hospital room. It was set up to hold two patients but thank God I was alone. She had me take off my shirt and put on a belly band and hospital gown. She let me keep on my jeans. She applied more warm gel to my tummy and strapped on a fetal heart beat monitor and a contraction monitor.

She inserted a catheter into my hand in case we needed to do an emergency C-section, I would be hooked up to I.V's. Then she left me alone. There I sat listening to the sound of hope, Chase's heart beat going thump thump thump thump thump.

I used this time to start calling my friends and family and try to get a hold of Jason. He wasn't answering his phone so I called my parents and I called my job.

Jason didn't get to the hospital until early afternoon. I ended up asking a neighbor to go to my house and wake him up.

We spent most of the day calling relatives and watching T.V waiting for something to happen. By early evening we were joined by Dr. Aroldi and Dr. Unger the neonatologist. He explained that a fetus has a very high rate of survival outside the womb after it reaches 28 weeks. My son was only 26 weeks. Our goal was to keep me pregnant until the 28-week mark and then evaluate from there.

Delivery at 28 weeks probably meant a surviving child but it did not necessarily mean a healthy child. If born that early, Chase would be at risk for blindness, birth defects and cerebral palsy.

As it already stood we didn't know if Chase suffered any brain damage or illness from the passing of Tyler. There is always a chance that the twin who dies can bleed out into the surviving twin and cause brain damage. A fetal M.R.I could tell us this for sure but we would have to go back To C.H.O.P to have this test. We are a pro-life family but even if we weren't 26 weeks is too late to get an abortion so the option was not on the table. We were in it now, for better or for worse. The only thing we could do was pray.

The plan was to keep me in the hospital until 28 weeks. I would have an ultrasound every morning. At 28 weeks, we would re-evaluate the situation.

The next two weeks seemed to drag on forever. I settled into a daily routine of wake up, have breakfast then an ultrasound. Shower, dress, and spend two hours calling/texting/Facebooking everyone I knew to report the news. Thankfully it was always good news. No sign of brain bleeds, strong heartbeat, looks healthy.

During these weeks, I learned who my true friends were. People who I never expected to come through came to visit me. They brought home made meals and presents but most importantly they brought themselves. They gave of their time to care for me.

On the other hand, some people who I expected would be there for me every second were not. Their absence will be forever noticed.

The worst night of my life was Christmas Eve 2010. An ice storm arrived and my husband was sick and didn't come visit me. My parents were already planning to come the next day. Everyone else I knew was at home with their family and I was alone in the hospital on Christmas Eve.

My dinner was grilled cheese which just made me sad and I kept picturing Tyler celebrating in heaven and that just put me over the edge. I spent the night crying and posting on the Facebook TTTS support sites.

About two days before New Year's Eve. I had passed our goal of 28 weeks and Chase seemed to be faring well the doctor let me go home for the remainder of the pregnancy provided I went to the Perinatologist office for daily ultrasounds and NST's.

I'll never forget how good it felt to go home on that

Thursday. The house smelled like a cinnamon candle and the Christmas tree was in good shape. My husband went shopping and filled the house with healthy foods. I was so glad to be able to sleep in my own bed.

My mom came up for New Years and I was tired and went to bed before midnight. I was awakened by the fireworks that our city lights at midnight and of course, I watched them through my bedroom window and cried and cried.

The ultrasounds continued to look good well into January. It wasn't until the last week of January, 2011 that Chase's cord blood flow numbers started to decrease every day. The first "bad" ultrasound occurred on a Thursday.

That Sunday my neighbor and friend Caren came over. She caught my husband and I in the middle of a fight. His argument was that every day a baby stays inside is good, and the earlier he is born the worse his health might be. My argument was that we had no idea what happened to Tyler and we were not getting daily monitoring at the time of his death. What if Chase was headed the same direction? What if I would have to "push out" two dead babies.

Caren understood how upset I was feeling and offered to come to the doctors with me on Monday so we could talk to the Perinatologist about an early delivery.

Dr. Bell agreed that it was time to end the pregnancy and that I would deliver that day.

Jason and I checked into the hospital late Monday afternoon. We tried to induce labor but I would not dilate. Around 9pm on Tuesday Chase's oxygen levels started to fail and I was brought in for an emergency C-section.

My Twins were born around 10 pm on Tuesday, January 25th. Chase was rushed to the NICU and I got to spend some time with Tyler. I wasn't prepared for how he would look and I didn't hold him. This is my biggest regret in life. I can't wait to hold him some day in heaven.

Chase

Chase spent almost 1 month in the NICU. He came home on February 18th 2010. He is now a healthy and happy little boy and is the light of our lives.

Cameron and Cole

Jodie Tummers

Jodie and I connected through the TTTS Survivors with Guardian Angels group. Someone asked me one time what that means. It means we have one twin that survived, and one twin that is the surviving twin's guardian angel. Just like Kathryn is to Charis, Cole is to Cameron.

Jodie's angel baby, Cole, also the recipient, like Kathryn developed hydrops (severe fluid buildup). I also learned something new while reading this story. Her surviving twin, Cameron, received a blood transfusion while in utero! It is so amazing how far medicine has come, but we have so far to go!

Jodie has done some amazing things since the loss of her twin... as you will read below! I cannot believe how much money she has raised for the hospital they were treated in! Jodie is also a wonderful writer, and blogs at Journey to Hope and Healing.

Cameron and Cole

My husband and I had always tossed around the ideal size of our family... he'd have had enough for a hockey line up if I'd been agreeable. I felt 3 was enough and had a 'plan' in mind as to when these babies should arrive. When our second son was about a year old I began to plan for baby 3 but that fall proved very stressful for us financially as my husband lost his job. By that spring we had decided that 2 children were enough and began talking about permanent birth control.

And then that July God intervened and I became pregnant. I was happy as I hadn't savoured all those 'last' moments with my second son as I believed I'd have another. On September 19th, I went for a scan for IPS screening, something I'd never done with the other pregnancies. I still remember the ultrasound tech saying 'I have some news for you...there's two babies in there'. I teared up as she showed me the two babies for the first time but it wasn't tears of sadness or even of joy... just of disbelief at the amazing thing that was happening.

My husband, was overjoyed at the news but I found

I was becoming increasingly overwhelmed with the thoughts of two newborns, no room in the house, double daycare etc. Everyone seemed to show this same excitement as my husband but where others pictured the excitement of two babies growing up together, I pictured the exhaustion of 2 newborns, the expenses and the stress. But that was the practical me talking... not the me who marveled at the uniqueness of our growing family, the joy of raising two identical little beings. It took me a bit to adjust but soon I, too, was so very excited. Within a few days of learning about our blessed babies, I began the hunt for strollers, for furniture and baby items. And I LOVED it... I loved telling people I was having twins. I told everyone I met...the more people I told, the happier I was about the two little lives growing inside of me. And with every punch and kick, every movement, even every ache and pain I would picture my identical twins in matching outfits smiling at the camera in my hands, playing together, laughing together, fighting with each other....and growing up together knowing each other better than any siblings really could. I was so excited about these babies growing inside of me.

    I read lots of books and websites on twins, joined an online support group and generally got informed. But I always avoided any reading on what could go wrong. I always asked if all was okay with my babies after each ultrasound and marveled at the images I saw each few weeks of my dear sweet babies. Ultrasounds did prove to be stressful though as each technician had a different feeling about the membrane dividing my babies...it was there/it wasn't there....no one seemed 100% sure but the feeling was that they were mono-di not mono-mono.

December 11th for me was a day like any other. I went to work and then left for an appointment late morning. We met with our OB and once again learned that our babies weren't cooperating for him to determine their sex. He told us we had a fine pair of babies in there and then asked when my next big scan was and told me it was good that it was that same day...perhaps his way of telling me he saw something that needed further investigation... I don't know. The ultrasound that afternoon was cancelled by the hospital but I was stubborn and insisted that they do it anyway since I was there. Thank goodness for my stubborn nature as during that ultrasound it became obvious that something wasn't right. After seeing 3 different people, I was left in the scan room for them to 'check to make sure they had everything'. After waiting for 20 minutes I began to suspect something wasn't right. As soon as my doctor came into the room I knew and I burst into tears. He tried to assure me all was well but the speed that I was being sent to see a specialist told me that this was very serious. I remember struggling to walk out of the hospital and make calls to husband, my mom and our babysitter. I was a mess and very hard to understand. I was so very scared for my babies.

We arrived in Toronto about 8:30 that night and were admitted. We had another ultrasound at about 9:00. This is where we found out that the babies were boys and the confirmation that our two babies had Twin to Twin Transfusion Syndrome. It was explained to us that one of our sons was transferring fluid to the other. This twin, Cameron, had no visible bladder and was stuck with no amniotic fluid around him. The other twin, Cole, seemed to be more affected. His cord was showing some reverse blood flow and there was some thickening seen in his heart. He had pockets of 8cm of fluid around him…the minimum needed to be considered TTTS. What I have learned in the 4+ years that TTTS has been part of our lives is that babies with only 8cm pockets are usually healthy, not often very affected by the polyhydramnios yet. I have also learned that normally in TTTS the donor baby is smaller than the recipient but our boys appeared to be about the same size, our recipient might be an ounce smaller. This gave the medical staff the assurance that our TTTS had only been occurring for a few days but also baffled them as to why his cord flow was so affected. The other discovery was that Cole's cord was inserted very poorly, 11cm away from the placental wall.

We made the decision to have surgery to try and save both of our boys the next day and returned to our room for a night and day of little sleep.

The next morning, we met Dr. Greg Ryan., we were amazed by his gentle nature and knew we were in great hands. We were warned that Cole was a sick baby, much sicker even then he'd been the night before. The ultrasound he performed then showed that there was now an increase to frequency of the reverse cord flow and the fluid pocket around him was up to 10cm and surgery was booked for as soon as possible. Nothing seemed real to us, as scared as we were, negative thoughts didn't cross our minds. Our focus was on our wonderful boys and all the fun we would have with them.

At 5:00 that afternoon another scan was performed just prior to the incision. Now Cole was showing an abdomen full of fluid.... definite hydrops, and this meant that TTTS was now at stage 4. During surgery it was discovered that there were 14 vessels connecting our boys through the placenta and of those 3 were quite large. These large ones were located right where the dividing membrane met the placenta and Dr. Ryan was forced to create a hole in this membrane to ensure all vessels were ablated. After the surgery was over, Dr. Ryan came to see us and explained what happened in the operating room, that he felt things went very well and what would happen the next day. He did tell us that Cole was very sick but we continued to feel optimistic about their future.

And then the world crashed around us the next morning. The day started out great. I felt strong movements and we had a good feeling about the fetal echocardiogram that we were scheduled to have later that morning. We went were taken to Sick Kids Hospital across the street and were excited to find out how both of our boys where doing. Expecting to hear from the doctor that both boys where going to be keeping me uncomfortable for the next thirteen weeks, our world came to a sudden and frightening halt.

The words "I'm sorry, your baby's heart isn't beating" will be forever etched in my brain. We were completely blown away and devastated. And still expected to lie still while the cardiologist checked out our surviving twin.

The walk back to our room at Sinai was the longest walk that we've ever made. It felt like that we were in a dream; I hoped I would wake up in my bed at home and wonder why I was in this awful nightmare. Once back in our room, we just sat there in a daze. Not knowing what to say or do for each other. We shed a lot of tears, both of sadness for Cole and of fear for Cameron. Dr. Ryan came to visit us, trying to comfort us at the same time explaining that he needed to do another ultrasound on Cameron. They needed to ensure he was ok and that the passing of his brother had not affected him. It quickly became apparent that they were not sure this was the case. He was showing signs of anemia and it took them hours to decide if this was serious enough to perform a blood transfusion. One of the doctors, one I quickly began to dislike, made the comment that they were trying to decide if they should do the blood transfusion because they might just be saving a very sick baby.

Thankfully Dr. Ryan had a much better outlook on things and he decided it was totally worth it and later that evening Cameron was given 40 cc's of blood via a very long needle inserted into my abdomen, through the wall of the uterus and into his umbilical cord. By the next morning, he was showing definite signs of improvement and by later that week, after an MRI and further ultrasound he was given a clean bill of health.

And me... well I spent most days in tears. I felt so much guilt at my reaction to the initial news of our twins and such devastation that I wasn't going to be raising my twins together after all. I found support on

Fetal Health's website as well as the Twin to Twin Transfusion Syndrome's message boards. It was amazing to talk to some of these other moms and to not feel so alone and yet at times it made me feel more confused and fearful as I learned increasingly more about TTTS and some of the things that others had done different that had seemingly saved their babies. Each day got a bit easier though celebrating Christmas just 12 days after losing Cole was one of the hardest things I've ever done. Dreams of matching clothes, holiday pictures and shared toys for our twins were shattered. I wondered how Christmas could ever be normal for me again.

On Jan. 3rd, I rolled over in bed and knew instantly that something was wrong. I went to my local hospital and they weren't sure what was going on but felt it wasn't a rupture of my membranes and sent me back home with the request that I come back for a full scan in the morning. By then we knew it was a rupture as the fluid loss had increased a lot. An Ambulance took me back to Toronto and met with Dr. Ryan again. Dr. Ryan told us that he expected our baby to be born in the next few days to one week. They were very concerned as he was just over 26 weeks but still measuring behind... more the size of a 24-weeker. They began to prepare me for the arrival of this micro preemie but it just didn't seem like my reality. We met with Dr. Ryan a few days after my water broke and after scanning me he asked me to sit up and chat.... We needed a birth plan. That was reality, and it scared me senseless...he really believed we were about to meet my sons. A few days later we toured the NICU and reality hit even harder. These little 650 gram babies on ventilators that gently shook the baby... no way, I could not do this, could not bear to see my son in that position.

One of the hardest things for me at that point was the loss of control I had over my life. I had big plans of how I would prepare for the birth of my boys. Research I planned to do on how to honour Cole, remember Cole and things I wanted to get...matching blankets, teddy bears etc. And now I was stuck in this bed in a city that I truly disliked and there was nothing I could do about it.

It is a testament to the strength and power of a guardian angel that Cameron held on for another almost 8 weeks before he made his arrival and that he required almost no interventions. I truly believe, having read all the medical reports and learning what I did in hospital that Cole was always meant to be Cameron's guardian angel. There is no medical reason that the symptoms that caused Cole's heart to fail and for him to be small in size (he had less than 25% share of the placenta and would for certain been labeled SIUGR had he survived TTTS and he had a severe velamentous cord insertion) didn't show themselves earlier in the pregnancy. I think Cole was doing his best to hide all that was wrong from everyone so that Cameron would be at a safe point before he journeyed home to be with God and took on the role of protector for Cameron and the rest of our family.

Cameron was born at 34 weeks weighing 4lbs 1.5 oz. He was at the 10th percentile for his gestational age making him borderline for IUGR as well. He had some serious contracture issues in his limbs from the lack of fluid to move and grow in and continued to struggle with weight gain until he was about 7 months old. He was in the care of a dietician for about 6 months and a physiotherapist for about 18 months.

He is now almost 4 years old and I often think that he has the strength, energy, love and zest for life of two boys...which would make sense since he as the soul of 2.

In the last few years many things have changed in my life. Upon leaving the hospital, just over 24 hours after learning that our precious son was gone, my husband and I discussed that we wanted to do something for Dr. Ryan and Mt. Sinai... to thank them, to honour Cole and to try to help ensure that other families didn't have to go through this heartache. I knew right then and there that I wanted to reach out to others going through TTTS and living in the aftermath. Eighteen months after Cameron and Cole were born we held our first fundraiser for Mt. Sinai. We raised over $4000 then and have raised over $14, 000. We have been able to meet with Dr. Ryan a few times and are working with him on a project to help families just diagnosed to connect with others and to get the resources and information they need. Each time we see him he tells us how amazed he is with Cameron. The first time he told me this he was very honest. He never felt Cameron would be as healthy and developmentally on track as he is. He had hope for Cameron but fully expected there to be delays, physical and developmental delays.

As for my early desire to reach out to others, that too has had a huge impact on my life. I have at least 200 Facebook friends that have experienced TTTS. I created 2 groups on Facebook to offer support and am active in numerous others. I work closely with a foundation called Fetal Health to support others and connect them with the places and people that can help them best.

All those things sound so positive and it might seem that my journey was just that, a positive growth. The fact is grieving took a lot out of me, it cost me friendships and it changed me forever. There were times where I felt like I was in a deep dark pit and could not find my way out. I had a belief in God right from the start and very, very slowly I began to turn that belief into faith, into a relationship with God. I seemed to find little bits of information here and there that gradually helped me grow a sense of hope for my future but it was a slow and painful journey at times.

The more I explored my faith the bigger my eyes became, the more in tune my ears became and the more enlightened my heart became. I had a great many questions and God always seemed to put something on my heart that would help to answer them. Eventually that hope turned to peace and a sense of acceptance. Around 2.5 years after the twins were born God lead our family to a new church and there I finally began to truly find answers to the questions and understand who Jesus really was. I realized that he had been there the whole time…sometimes I fought him and his desire to help and comfort me but he never gave up on me. And so I gave myself to him and have found what I can only describe as a peaceful acceptance of all that has happened and a knowledge that where there is sorrow there is also joy, where one door closes he opens another for me. To be who God wanted me to be I had to experience trials and heartache and I can say with complete confidence that it was all worth it.

At one point at the start of this journey I had said I wanted to turn back time and change everything. I'm know now that I don't feel the same way. Don't get me wrong, I wish that I could go back and prevent Cole from losing his life to TTTS. But doing that would change everything and I know that this is who I am meant to be. Doing that would change my relationships, would remove so many amazing people who I have never even met in person from my life. Doing that would change my relationship with Christ because I wouldn't have had the same reason to rely on him.

This journey has shown me so many amazing things and none of it would be a part of our lives if we changed everything. And if we changed everything then the Cameron we have grown to know, to love, to admire might not be a part of our lives either. And if we changed everything then our little Cole who has given us so many moments that have taken our breath away without ever having taken a breath might not be a part of our lives either ...

... because without Cole there is no Cameron and without Cameron there is no Cole.

Micah and Spencer

Melissa Johnson

What struck me when I first opened the email from Melissa with her story was that the ultrasound picture she included is almost EXACTLY the same as one that I have of my girls... heads right next to each other, just hanging out! And, of course, we both delivered two live babies and had to say goodbye to one shortly after. I felt immediately bonded to Melissa. Her story is an amazing story of faith and love, and she does an excellent job of really portraying and explaining how TTTS changes us.

Micah and Spencer

When people hear about TTTS experiences, I think they expect it to be a story with a beginning, middle, and end. The truth is, there is a beginning, but the story never ends. TTTS is life-altering. Regardless of quality of care, regardless of outcome--all survivors, some survivors, no survivors--it changes your life: it changes you.

There is nothing else in the world like being told you are having twins (or multiples). As soon as you get over the shock, joy sets in and you start making plans and start dreaming dreams, and you feel special. You're having twins! And then TTTS tears the joy away, and it makes you afraid to make plans and dream dreams, because now your only hope, your only prayer is that your babies will live. That they will survive long enough to hold them in your arms. Beyond that is too painful to even think about. And for those that are never diagnosed, they don't even get that transition. They go straight from dreaming of hands full to weeping with hands and arms empty.

Regardless of the beginning of the story, TTTS continues to be a part of your life, for the rest of your life, because it alters the way you look at things. It alters what is important to you, and it changes your dreams, plans, hopes, and fears. Your innocence is gone--and will be forever.

The following is the beginning of our story and how our innocence was--and continues to be--changed.

My story begins with a prayer. I had three boys and

knew I wanted more children, and I had an overwhelming desire to have twins. I know, crazy! But I did, and I prayed and prayed and prayed to please let me have twins. I was just a little (or maybe a lot) obsessed, and the desire just kept weighing on my mind. Finally, I said, "Heavenly Father, I really want twins, but nevertheless, Thy will be done." And then I felt peace, and I knew that regardless of what happened, it would be God's will. And it would be okay.

Well, I got pregnant. And my pregnancy was different enough from my other pregnancies (don't worry, no details) that I was sure it was twins. I didn't want to hope too much, but I was reading about twins, looking things up on the Internet about twins, and just felt like it was twins. We had our first scan at 12 weeks. The day before had been a rough one (three little boys can be overwhelming sometimes), and I convinced myself that there was no way I was having twins because I couldn't even handle the three I already had. So, my doctor starts scanning and says, "are you sitting down?", to my husband, "because there are two babies in there". All I could do was laugh.... We were having twins!

We went out in the parking lot and called our parents right away. I started making plans and figuring out how to arrange the house, and where to keep diapers, and play sets and everything we would need. I started thinking about freezer meals and mom and mom-in-law coming to help. I thought about a million things all at once, and over and under and around and through it all was this tremendous joy. I went out that day and bought a book about twins. And then I went home and read it. I remember reading a short page and a half about TTTS and remarking to my husband "we really don't want to get this" and reading out loud the part about 5% survival rate with no treatment...

Fast forward six weeks; with all my previous pregnancies, I "popped" around 16-18 weeks along, so when I suddenly was bigger, and growing out of all my maternity clothes I thought nothing of it. I went to buy extra large size maternity clothes (normally I wear small or medium). The lady at the store said usually with a twin pregnancy you only go up one size. My response was "well I'm only half way along and I'm not fitting anything". I thought she just didn't know what she was talking about. I remember going to a family reunion with a cousin who was due the exact same day as me and being proud of how big my tummy was compared to hers. A week later we saw the Perinatologist (my doctor tried to get me in earlier but he was completely booked- he only came up to our hospital twice a month, and his office was 1 1/2 hours away). So, I said we could drive down there. I didn't know anything was wrong, I just knew that my doctor had told his nurse to book me an appointment "the earlier the better".

I went in for our 20-week scan, so looking forward to finding out the gender of our babies. I remember feeling like one of the babies was pushing against my ribs. It felt exactly like it did when my 9lb9oz 22" long baby did when he would stretch out and push his feet against my ribs. I kept pushing my stomach down- it hurt. When I mentioned it to the ultrasound technician she said "actually it's all this extra fluid". And then when she was done she said "I have a lot more respect for you, I thought you were just being wimpy, but you have as much fluid as someone who is 8 1/2 months pregnant"... I still didn't get it. And then the Perinatologist took us into a special conference room, and started drawing diagrams, and explaining that our boys (yep, two more boys!) were sick, and there wasn't a cure, but there were a couple of different options for treatment. We were in shock. He made an appointment for us to come back in two days (at a different hospital with a different Perinatologist, since of course his hospital wasn't a participating provider). As an aside, that one scan and appointment cost us more than everything else that was to come combined.

So, we came back. Our boys were re-checked, they were staying stable at a high-level I. Our doctors, who I loved, again went over all our options (do nothing, serial amniocentesis, and surgery) and the expected outcomes. Basically, at that time, doing nothing meant a 5% chance of any survival. And trying some treatment gave you a 60% chance of bringing both babies home to an 80% chance of bringing one baby home, with laser surgery having a slightly higher rate of survival. Our doctors suggested that we call around to the different treatment centers that did the laser surgery and consult with them about our case before it became an emergency. At the time, there only were five centers (not five doctors) in all of the United States that had completed more than 50 surgeries. We talked to multiple doctors, and we decided because of location to family, we would fly out to UCSF to be evaluated. I had to have a signed note from my doctor saying that I was only 28 weeks, just in case the airline wouldn't let me on the plane...

    I flew out on a Thursday, and spent all day Friday having tests run by multiple specialists. At the end of the day, we had gone from a level I to a level II, and the surgeon suggested we have the surgery. We agreed and so the following Tuesday they performed fetalscopic laser ablation surgery. My boys shared the placenta pretty equally, and my donor even showed signs of improvement while I was still on the operating table.

The doctors did say that the recipient's heartbeat had dropped to around 60 for less than five minutes, and we might want to have an MRI performed. We decided not to because it would not change our plan at all--which was to keep those babies cooking as long as possible. Before we left he said he thought we had an 80% chance of taking both babies home. My happy moment in church that following Sunday was that "I was home, and so were both of my babies"- meaning they had survived the surgery, and were still fighting.

Things went well for the next two weeks. Fluid levels looked good, hearts looked good, etc. And then three weeks after surgery, I went in for my weekly check-up, and my donor's bladder wasn't visible, and there were membranes floating around. So, TTTS had returned, and it was possible they were now mono-mono, meaning, they now shared the same sac. They told me to go home and come back Monday. I came back Monday with a bag packed- assuming I would be put on hospital bed rest. I had just hit 25 weeks the day before.

They did an ultrasound and were able to determine that only my recipients sack had been shredded, so they were still separate, but my donor still had very little fluid, and no visible bladder. While they were performing the NST the technician noticed that I was having contractions- I was in labor and didn't even know it! I was expecting to be admitted- but not because I was in labor! I was not supposed to be having these babies yet and it scared me.

I was sent to labor and delivery, where at 9:00 that night they were finally able to stop my labor. Once I was stabilized and all the doctors consulted--including the surgeon at UCSF--they determined the only thing left to do was monitor the babies, and as soon as they would be healthier outside than in, we would deliver. I had ultrasounds and NST's every day during the week, and heartbeat checks every four hours. Our goal was to make it to 28 weeks, where our boys had a good chance of surviving without complications. I was on bed rest for three weeks, and at 28 weeks exactly I went in to labor that wouldn't be stopped. I had decided I wanted to deliver vaginally, not knowing that delivering by C-section was the safer option. There was so little information at that time: we found two websites total that talked about TTTS at all, and even on those sites, the information was minimal. This was before Facebook: we thought we were pretty on top of things because we had a blog going just for our boys :-), but I digress.

So, I was in labor, and things just weren't progressing- my recipient's head couldn't engage because there was so much fluid. So they decided to break my water. And flooded everything! And then my recipient's heart rate dropped a bit, so they decided they should do a C-section. At that point things happened fast and got a little fuzzy for me. I remember them poking my belly and asking me if I could feel it, and I could (I had an epidural, but at a low strength), so they pumped me up again, and then everyone was rushing around, and I could still feel things, so they put something directly into the line. They had me switch beds (because mine was soaking wet) and I remember seeing blood on my hands. Everyone was rushed, They rolled me into the operating room, i could hear the doctor giving orders, they poked me again and I could still feel it, so they put me completely under.

When I woke up I was told that my placenta had abrupted, and I was hemorrhaging. I had one and almost two blood transfusions. Micah, our recipient, was 3 lbs. Spencer, our donor, was 1lb 9 oz. They were born at 1:34 and 1:35 PM on March 5, 2007. Spencer had to have a blood transfusion, and Micah had to have blood removed soon after they were born. That night, when I was able to leave the recovery room, they wheeled me on my bed into the NICU where I saw my boys for the first time. I barely had energy to raise my head, but I saw my boys, and my heart melted. They were so tiny, so fragile, and so perfect! I loved them even more than I already had. One of my prayers had been answered- they were alive. (Micah and then Spencer).

Three days later, I was so relieved because my milk had finally come in. I was going back to my room to pump, and the nurse called and said, "You should come back. Spencer is having a hard time. And call your husband: he needs to be here." We lived two hours away from the hospital. My husband was home working but was planning to come in later that day for a care conference with the doctors/nurses/etc. So my mom wheeled me back to the NICU and I went to my little Spencer's side. He was almost black. He had had an episode where they had to work over him for 15+ minutes and ended up giving him a drug that effectively paralyzed him so he would stop fighting the ventilator and start breathing again.

As I sat there with my finger on my son, I prayed and prayed. "Dear God, I need a miracle, please help him to hold on until his Dad gets here, please, help him recover, I'm not ready to say good-bye yet, please, please, I need a miracle. Please God, not yet. Not yet." That prayer was answered with a yes, and Spencer stabilized. That afternoon, after my husband arrived and spent some time with both of our boys, we went to our first care conference. My husband refers to that afternoon as the "Info-mercial from Hell" ("But wait:

there's more!").

The neonatologist working with my boys, the two nurse managers, the two nurses, and the social workers assigned to my boys, plus me, my mom, and my husband, and possibly my father-in-law (?) were all crammed into a conference room, where they proceeded to list everything going wrong with my little babies. It kept going and going and going. We'd think they were done and then we'd hear another "and". They said that their hearts and lungs were both failing, and on top of that they had extensive brain damage (PVL and brain bleeds in both boys). After they were done I said, "So if they get better they are going to be handicapped?" (Or something like that), and they said, "We don't think they are going to get better. And if--if--they do, it is possible they would never be able to leave the hospital. They would need 24 nursing supervision, you need to seriously consider letting them go: both of them." The doctors said that frankly, they were completely shocked by the results of the brain ultrasounds.

My sweet little boys, had been dealing with TTTS for 10 weeks now, they had a short reprieve after the surgery, but TTTS and a traumatic birth had made its mark, and we didn't know what we were going to do. We were completely devastated. We had been prepared for the possibility of one or both of them having issues. We were in no way prepared to hear that they were most likely going to die. My husband and I went back to my room that night and wondered how in the world we were supposed to decide what to do. We had faith that our boys could be healed, and yet we also wanted to show God that we had faith in Him, and His will for our boys. So, our prayer became this- "Dear Father in Heaven, we love our boys, and do not want to let them go, but if you need them, that is okay too. So, if it is all right with Thee, we are going to hang on to our boys as long as they stay the same, or get better. If they worsen then we will know they are being called home, and we will let them go."

The next day, the neonatologist said "I got a second opinion of the head ultra-sounds, and the second opinion wasn't as harsh as the first, I suggest you hold off on making a decision. We will run all the tests again next Monday and have another care conference after that." We spent the weekend sitting beside our boys, reaching fingers in to rest lightly on their little heads, and introducing them to family and friends who traveled long distances to meet these little boys who might not be with us much longer. I remember the first time I could reach my arms in the incubator and hold my little Spencer up while they changed his bedding underneath, I was filled with overwhelming love, and felt love back from him. One time as we were sitting watching, Spencer had his eyes open, and he was just looking at us, telling us as best he could that he loved us.

I could do the same with Micah, and oh it was marvelous to feel each of their weight in my arms.

The tests were run Monday, and a care conference scheduled for Tuesday. Before I had left for the hospital Tuesday morning, my husband called: the doctors had called him and Spencer's bowel had perforated in the night. Given how sick he already was, there was nothing they could do. Our little boy was dying. On the drive to the Hospital I watched out the window, praying "God, I know he can be healed, I know thou hast the power to bind up the holes. I know miracles are possible. But if not, if he is being called home, then I give him to Thee, Father in heaven. I am giving him to you. Please take care of him for me." I hurried to the hospital and to my sweet little boy. Seth was again at home, two hours away and the doctors kept asking when he would get there, worried that Spencer would pass before he got there. Spencer held on long enough for his daddy to get there, and long enough for the nurses to unhook him from everything, clean him up, and bring him to us. He died after just a few minutes in our arms. We had eight precious days with him. We held him in our arms for the first time, told him how much we loved him, kissed him, took some pictures, and cried.

And then, concerned for our other son, we decided to go ahead and see what the doctors had to say.

So, care conference number two: "Micah is probably just a few days behind his brother. You should really consider just letting him go with his brother." We sat and talked about it for hours. If the doctors were right and he was going to die anyway, why prolong the pain? Why put their brothers through the pain of losing one brother, and then a few days later, losing another? If we were going to have to say good-bye twice, let's just do it now.

But what if- what if the doctors were wrong? Can we really handle letting him go? We just didn't know. We felt like either way we decided would be okay: not right or wrong. And so, not wanting to wait, and then go through all of this again, we made the decision to let him go. And we went to visit him, and we were again unsure. He looked like there was nothing wrong (other than prematurity), so my wise husband said, "If we don't know for sure, then we should wait to make a decision." And so we did. That night we told our three older boys that Spencer was very sick, and had gone home to Heavenly Father and Jesus. We had made an effort beforehand to teach them about God, and when we were first diagnosed, about heaven. The next morning the doctor called for permission to perform a simple procedure (having to do with his IV), I felt like if we were going to let him go it would be pointless. I looked at my husband and said, I think we need to stick to our original game plan, if he gets worse we'll let him go, if not we hold on. He agreed.

That Saturday day we laid our precious child to rest- it was the only time I saw my husband cry.

And then started a three-month-long NICU ordeal. After holding steady for three long weeks, my Micah started improving. My husband and oldest son stayed at home for school and work, and I and my other two sons lived with my in-laws during the week since they were closer to the hospital and so my mother-in-law could watch my two boys while I went in to the hospital every day to be with Micah.

On the weekends, we would go home to give my children a sense of normalcy and so we could be together. We would go to church Sunday, and then my husband would drive down to spend a few hours with Micah and then come back. Then on Monday, we would do it all over again. My in-laws would usually go in on Saturday so Micah had someone visit him every day. He was on the ventilator for six weeks. It was just over six weeks before I could hold my baby in my arms, outside of the incubator. He was on CPAP for two weeks after that, and when he made it to oxygen, it was discovered he had hydrocephalus and had to have brain surgery to place a catheter and a tube draining the fluid his brain couldn't absorb due to his brain bleeds from his brain to his abdominal cavity. He was just two months old, and still six weeks shy of his due date.

Up to this point, Micah had not been able to eat anything by mouth. I wanted to try breastfeeding him. We tried, and the doctors were so kind. They let me discover on my own timeline that my little boy was not capable of getting food that way. They wanted to place a G-tube, but I wanted to try a bottle before that, so I asked what a realistic period would be, and then requested I have that much time to try a bottle. So, with much coaching from nurses and the Occupational therapists, we tried the bottle. And he did it! I had to count sucks, and remind him to breathe, and it took over an hour sometimes, but he did it! A week later, 96 days after he was born, my Micah came home. His official diagnoses were/are Cerebral Palsy, Optic Nerve Hypoplasia (his optic nerves were smaller than they should have been- which meant he was visually impaired), chronic lung disease, reflux, and medically fragile (susceptible to getting sick). The neurologists said that Micah would probably never walk, never talk, with a more than 85% chance he would never progress beyond infant stage. Despite everything, he is the happiest little blessing in our family. Micah gets joy out of life, and shares it with us. He has proven the doctors wrong by living, and is slowly proving them wrong by continuing to progress, slowly but surely.

All of the dreams that existed before TTTS are dead now. Our hopes, our dreams, our outlook on life has all been altered. We have been altered. It is now six years since my twins were born, and TTTS continues to shape our lives, as each day we miss our sweet Spencer, and each day we care for Micah. However, there is one thing that TTTS has not, cannot change. And that is how much we love our boys, our identical twins, Micah and Spencer.

Crew and Dex

Megan Bradshaw

If you are a TTTS parent and you don't know about Teeny Tears, you need to learn about it. It's a fabulous service organization to anyone who has lost a baby... you'll read more farther down. Teeny Tears was founded and is run by a TTTS mama – Megan, mother to Crew and Dex.

Megan is an incredible and beautiful, strong woman, and someone I am proud to call a friend. In the past few years, Teeny Tears has exploded across the United States.

Megan posted a quote from one of the Teeny Tears representatives who attended a bereavement conference in Chicago.

"Being at the conference was a wonderful chance to hear from hospitals that were already using Teeny Tears diapers about how much they were appreciated by the staff and the families. The nurses loved having something to offer the families that was handmade with such love. The conference was also a great chance to introduce new hospitals to the diapers. Nothing is as convincing as seeing how truly small the diapers are and touching them to feel how soft they are for delicate skin." ~Katrina

After Kathryn died, I began sewing diapers for this project, and we donate them to the local hospitals. It was such a healing act for me. I encourage you to look it up as well.

Crew and Dex

In the summer of 2008, our family received the exciting and surprising news that we were expecting twins! Knowing that we were now involved in a high-risk pregnancy, I hopped onto the internet and learned all I could. In the back of my mind all I kept thinking was, "people have twins every day! This is not scary; this is exciting!"

Early in November, when I was only 28 weeks along, my water broke in the middle of the night. After calling one of our good neighbors to stay with our children, we raced to the hospital. At first the nurses couldn't find any heartbeats, but that didn't seem terribly unusual or alarming because they were very young and very small babies. After they had given me all the medicines in their arsenal to stop my labor, they became more serious about finding heartbeats. They found one tiny, weak heartbeat and it was failing quickly. They rushed me across the hall to the operating room and brought my sons into the world 4 minutes later through an emergency C-section.

When I awoke from the general anesthesia several hours later, my whole world had changed. Our son Crew was 1 pound 8 ounces, the size of a dollar bill. He had been born without a heartbeat, but was quickly resuscitated. Two more minutes and we would have lost him. As it was, he had a very tumultuous 3 months in the NICU, camping out on death's door more times than we care to count. Today our little survivor attends special needs preschool. He started walking and talking this past summer and is a great blessing to our family.

Our son Dex was 2 pounds 1 ounce. It was my husband's greatest sorrow to tell me that our little one did not survive his journey. He had passed away minutes to hours before birth TTTS. I learned later that my doctor had suspected that we were developing this disease, but hadn't wanted to alarm me, so failed to mention it during our final ultrasound appointment. He also did not send us to a Perinatologist, or mention the possibility when I went into false labor twice in the weeks preceding the delivery of our sons. I had asked about the possibility of TTTS during every ultrasound appointment... except our final ultrasound at 25.5 weeks. It was the one time I did not ask about it. My doctor did not understand the urgency of proper diagnosis and intervention. Years later I learned that I had been exhibiting all the classic symptoms of TTTS on a rampage. In the end, we had TTTS, placental abruption, and ruptured separation sacs. I thought I was just 5 foot 1 and having twins. Little did I know what a dangerous train wreck was going on inside.

Dex was placed in my arms wearing this beautiful handmade gown that was appropriately sized for his tiny body. The bereavement specialist at the hospital took hand molds and feet molds so that we could always remember how small he had been. They took beautiful pictures of him that we count among our greatest treasures today. They were even able to take a few pictures of our sons together in Crew's incubator, the only photos we will ever have of them together outside of the womb.

Meeting Dex in person was one of the most beautiful experiences of my life. I felt him the moment his body entered the room and holding him in my arms the first time was like a healing salve for my broken heart. I'll never be able to explain it perfectly, but the closest I can come is to say that I just felt an overwhelming sense of peace and hope and love from my Heavenly father. He was so beautiful. His spirit stayed with us throughout the day, giving us comfort and letting us know without question that he loved us, he knew us, he claimed us as his parents, and that things had turned out exactly as they were supposed to, no matter how we got there.

I don't wish to give the impression that my heart wasn't completely broken, because the truth is that I didn't know how I could bear to live without him. There were so many moments of anguish, nights that I was afraid to fall asleep, tortured thoughts of how we could have saved him with earlier intervention.

Sometimes the miracle is in the miraculous healing of a child against all odds, as we received with Crew. And sometimes the miracle is in the healing of our hearts when trials and tragedy strike, crushing our expectations and threatening our faith.

As we came closer and closer to Dex and Crew's third birthday, I began searching for a project that would **honor Dex's memory** and give purpose to my grief. I was looking for something economical, meaningful, and within my limited sewing abilities.

I would make tiny little diapers for stillborn micro preemie infants and those that pass away in the NICU.

We launched **Teeny Tears**.

Approximately 26,000 children are stillborn in the United States every year, about 1 in 160 births. Another 19,000 children die within the first 28 days of life. A significant number of these angels are preemie or micro preemie infants. The littlest angels are so small that even the very tiniest Pampers NICU diaper is far too large for them. Besides that, their skin is so delicate that commercial diapers are very damaging.

Our volunteers donate to hospitals and bereavement support organizations at no charge. These small diapers fit angels between 18 and 23 weeks gestation. The large ones fit angels between about 24 and 30 or 32 weeks. The need for these diapers is enormous and endless. Gone are the days when angel babies must be left with naked bums because there is nothing suitable. No longer must nurses try to fashion a "diaper" out of cotton balls and tape. Our little diapers offer dignity and modesty to the tiniest angel babies. We provide two diapers per family, so that the parents don't have to choose whether to keep the diaper in a memory box or to bury the diaper with their child. This way they can do both.

Grieving parents often feel very lost, alone, and confused. Every special effort to honor their loss goes a long way. It is very difficult for a family to say goodbye to their child before they got to say a decent hello. These diapers, made with love, tell parents that someone understands that their child existed, that they are special, loved, real, and that they matter. The love that goes into these diapers tells a grieving parent that someone understands that their loss is tremendous. Because "a person's a person, no matter how small."

As you can imagine, November is always a tender time of year for our family. The year we launched Teeny Tears was the first November that I didn't spend the first half of the month hiding under my covers in bed, eating chocolate leftover from Halloween. As I sewed for angel families, I felt close to my son and my heart was filled with love and a peace I didn't know was possible.

Teeny Tears is my way to make sure that Dex and all of his angel friends are remembered. It has been an unexpectedly joyful and healing endeavor and I have met some of the most caring and generous people along the way. Many of our volunteers are angel families themselves, some of them still the walking wounded. As they participate in serving others in a similar plight, a miracle happens. They find their own sorrows lessened and their hearts begin to heal. Joy is found and lives are changed.

What began as a personal labor of love for the angel families at my friend's local hospital in Washington and then ours in Utah has caught on like wildfire within the bereavement community. We have a busy Facebook group filled with volunteers across the United States as well as in Canada, Australia, and New Zealand who are gathering their families, friends, neighbors, and churches to serve Heavenly Father's tiniest children and their bereaved families. We even made our first delivery to a hospital in Guatemala.

As an inexpensive, simple, unique, educational, and meaningful service opportunity, our diapers are being sewn by families, sewing clubs, youth groups, Eagle Projects, Angel Mother grief support organizations, and churches of all religious denominations. We encourage our volunteers to donate within their local communities and we also match volunteers with hospitals all over the country on our growing waiting list. Grandmothers are digging their flannel scraps out of storage, families are repurposing old receiving blankets and shopping yard sales for fabric remnants. And we know when all the fabric sales are going on!

To date, our volunteers have donated more than 21,000 diapers to grieving angel families across the world. While I wish no one ever needed our diapers, I am pleased that there is something that we can try to do for these families to let them know that they are not alone.

Crew just turned 4 years old. He is charming, sweet, and far too small for his age. While he continues to be challenged by the lingering effects of TTTS, we are so lucky to have him with us.

Walker and Willis

Brooke Myrick

We conclude the single survivor's section with Walker and Willis. This is a story that is very close to my heart. I feel so many of the same emotions and sentiments that Brooke describes in her story. When I look at her surviving twin, I feel that it is a glimpse into my future. It saddens me to think of my Charis in several years when she is old enough to understand what she has lost, what she will never know.

Brooke and I have become friends as we've shared about our loss. She has written a very beautiful tribute to her boys.

Walker and Willis

This time of year brings me back and always has. Six

years seems like yesterday; then again it seems so far away at the same time. I remember walking around at the fair wanting to throw up with all the mixed smells of greasy food. I knew I was pregnant but boy was I in for a surprise. A surprise and events that would change me. Events that would devastate my life while at the same time bring joy into my life. That joy is a little boy named Walker.

I was in love that fall. We hadn't really dated that long just since March, but I knew that he was the one. In September I got a ring and a few days later found out I was pregnant. We decided to get married on October 20 the same day as our first ultrasound. We decided just to go to courthouse since it was easier and less expensive. October came with a chill. I thought how I had this wonderful life and would have the most wonderful family. On that day, I lay down on that ultrasound table and watched as I saw one baby and she moved it over and there were two! She said, "It's twins!" My mom is a twin and Michael's grandma is a twin. Needless to say, we all were over the moon excited. Nothing could bring me down or so I thought. We went to courthouse telling anyone we saw how we just found out we were having twins.

I continued to work and was sick and barely gained any weight. I always asked if this ok and was continuously told that everything was fine. At almost 20 weeks we had an ultrasound and found out they were two boys. I was so happy! I had always wanted a little boy and now I would have two! Michael was happy too. And in that moment, I knew that all I wanted was my little boys and I would be complete. Looking back at my records at this ultrasound Willis was already starting to fall behind walker. Why this didn't raise any concerns (considering they were sharing a placenta) I'll never know.

On January 3, on a cold dreary day as I recall, I went to the doctor for an ultrasound to measure my cervix to ensure I wasn't showing signs of going into labor early. That day would change my life. It is by far the worst day I've had in my life and I pray every day I never experience one worse.

I can't explain it but I had a bad feeling about the ultrasound. I felt something just wasn't right. After a few minutes the sonographer told me my twin A my precious Willis was gone. He no longer had a heartbeat. In a moments time my world came crashing down. I went from thinking I had two healthy babies to "one of your babies is gone." All I could do is cry. I was in shock I had a million whys racing through my head and how.

All I heard that day was twin B no longer has a heartbeat. In the days that followed I started to think about the other half of her sentence that day "the other twin looks fine but I will go get the doctor". It was hard not having Willis but I had to fight for my little fighter Walker. He was still fighting for me and I had to fight for him. And God was fighting for both of us.

How could they be fine and now one is gone?

I was naive. In years since that day I've often wondered why my twins weren't being watched closer. I just don't believe it's right to go four or five weeks in between ultrasounds with twins especially identical an sharing a placenta. And I've made it my lifelong mission to make awareness.

I wish someone had told me about the risks involved. It honestly probably wouldn't have changed my outcome. It was so early on. And although there is a laser surgery that can be performed I had an anterior placenta which would have made it hard. Also, Walker was in distress.

Whatever connections they had once Willis passed it didn't affect Walker anymore thank goodness. I'm not sure we would have qualified for the surgery.

I prayed and prayer and prayed for those babies. I know the God I serve would have given me an opportunity to save them if that had been his will. It doesn't mean I don't sometimes get angry that my boys weren't being watched like they should have. Those were my babies. I wish I had known they were sick.

We were sent to specialist the following day. And in walked this tall black man with Jamaican accent. His name was Dr. Bailey and it was instant love at first site. Oh, how I love that man to this day. He comforted me and told me it was nothing that I did wrong and he told me Walker looked good.

He told me right off that the boys were identical which is something my regular doctor never told me. He explained that identical twins often share connections in the placenta and if they aren't balanced just right can cause problems or death of one or both twins.

The most heartbreaking thing to me was that thy estimated Willis had been gone for two weeks or so. It broke my heart and I remember feeling weird and sick a few days after Christmas that year and personally I believe that was around the time he passed.

I felt guilty. What kind of mother was I to walk around and not know her son was gone? Of course, I realize it wasn't my fault but I couldn't help but have those thoughts.

I was sent home and had weekly ultrasounds with my regular OB. It didn't take long for him to realize Walker was no longer growing like he should. He wasn't gaining weight anymore. He was diagnosed with IUGR. They did an ultrasound test on him at the hospital. He was barely moving around any.

I got a call that afternoon to come to the hospital with my bags where I would be transferred to Huntsville to stay until delivery. I was sent by ambulance. I still remember how scared I was. I was 28 weeks. I was afraid my Walker wouldn't survive if taken this early.

Dr. Bailey came in that night and prayed with me and my family. He explained what would happen if Walker was born this early and his chances were good. He did an ultrasound and said he would do another one the next day and if Walker didn't look any better he would take him the next night.

It was a Wednesday night. I know of four or five churches who prayed for us that night. I had friends praying and friends of friends praying. And low and behold when he did that ultrasound the next night Walker was bouncing around all over the place. He said Walker looked like a different baby from the night before. He said we had gained another day. We would continue to be monitored all day and night. He let me off for a shower and that was it.

He did ultrasounds every few days. Days turned into weeks and a few weeks down the road on March 6 he came in to do an ultrasound. He asked how many weeks was I today and I said 32. He said, "I think we will take them to tonight." I called Michael at work. Everyone headed up that way. After what seemed like an eternity my precious Walker would come into the world where he could be fed better. And my oh it broke my heart to part with my Willis. I wanted to just carry him around forever with me.

At eleven that night, they pushed me back. I was so nervous. Within thirty minutes I was hearing the cries of my Walker. It was the sweetest sound I had ever heard. I was so thankful and still am.

But oh, how I wished it was two little baby boys crying. Walker was carried to NICU by Michael. He was breathing on his own. He weighed just under three pounds. They asked did I want to see Willis.

I wasn't ready yet. The first time I saw my son I wanted it to be our time. I didn't want all the nurses and doctors watching. The next day I was on morphine and felt out of it. I didn't want to see Willis this way either. I asked for him on that second day. I went to see Walker in NICU and broke down. I told my nurse I want to go back to my room and see my other baby. I remember seeing the people lined up to see their babies as she wheeled me out. I was crying so hard. I never liked crying in front of people but I didn't care in the moment.

She brought my precious angel to me. He was so beautiful and tiny. He looked just like walker. I loved to hold his little hand. I knew in those moments I spent with him he was with me in that room. I think he's always with me. That same night me and Michael saw him again together. We dressed him in his little gown and took some pictures. I now regret that we didn't take more. I don't think I could have ever took enough of him.

I held him and kissed him and I thought he was just perfect. I thought they both were.

The nurses in the NICU talked about how cute Walker was. When me and Michael walked up beside his bed and he would hear us talking those little eyes would start blinking open. I knew Walker missed his brother. I also think Walker knew how much we all prayed for him. I hated leaving him in the NICU even though he had wonderful nurses. I cried wishing I could be there with him all the time and I cried because I missed his brother.

I hope people realize how very thankful I was and am for Walker but one child does not replace another. We will always feel a void for the son who is not here. Although we do rejoice in the fact that we know he is in peace and is happy. Oh I believe that God and Jesus takes good care of the babies in heaven. I just love the song "Jesus loves the little children."

I like to share my story to raise awareness. I know doctors get busy but every patient should get the care they deserve. I think we need laws setting certain standards of care in OB as far as ultrasounds are concerned. I understand the cost may be one thing involved but I know women who got ultrasound every week or two week because their doctor cared enough to watch those babies.

If one doctor can do it why can't they all? Once somebody's child is gone you can't replace it. My outcome would probably not have been any different because of how small Willis was when he passed but there are women out there whose outcome could change according to how the doctors handled their care.

I believe my Willis is happy and if more babies could be saved by our story I know he is so happy about that. Sometimes I feel like Willis is telling me to chill out that its ok. The way Walker does when he says, "Mom it's ok."

I have had two more kids since my twins and I love them very much too. I know I wouldn't be the mother I am today if not for all I went through with the twins. I thank God every day that on that cold January day there was still a heartbeat left. That little boy kept me going. He keeps me going along with Jolie and Cooper. I'm so blessed. To be the mother of four beautiful children.

As I write this tears stream down my face. It was all l so traumatic and at the same time beautiful because it's the story of my twins, Walker and Willis.

Yes, I am still a mother of twins. No I don't get to dress them up alike and have to try to tell them apart but that does not mean I did not have twins. I'll never forget the pain of seeing Walker birth certificate where the women listed under plurality that it was a single birth. Well she didn't hear the last from my family. My sister Sarah called for me to question it. I was afraid to call myself because I knew I would get upset on the phone.

A few days before Christmas the year after Walker was born I received an amended birth certificate from Montgomery and it listed Walker as a surviving twin.

I could never have made it through without God. "What a friend we have in Jesus all our sins and griefs to bear. What a privilege to carry everything to God in prayer.

It is my goal that there is more awareness and understanding with all types of pregnancy or infant loss. Or just grieving in general.

The loss of a twin presents a very unique type of loss because here you are raising a constant reminder of your loss. I wouldn't have it any other way of course. Of course, I am so glad I haven Walker but as he grows and with every milestone it's a reminder of what I'm missing. It's bittersweet and can drain you dry.

All pregnancy losses are painful though and I don't think a woman ever gets past it fully. I was told throughout the rest of pregnancy with Walker to just try and focus on Walker. Can you imagine carrying around your deceased child and being told pretty much that I wasn't supposed to worry or think about him? He was my son and I wanted him here.

I understand many things said to me was meant in my best interest but sometimes it's just best not to speak if you're not sure what to say. This is not something I will ever get over. My family will not be complete until we are in heaven together.

No, I'm not a depressed person. I am a grieving mother who will always miss her son. And I do not believe grieving for Willis negatively affects my other children. They need to know its ok to grieve and be upset about their brother. They will hurt and miss him too. I can't explain how much the support I have gotten has meant. The kinds words and the mention of my son's name means so much.

I used to think if I posted pics of his grave or speak of him people will think I'm wanting attention. Then I decided that if anyone did think that they must not really know me. I speak of him and post pics of him because he is a part of my family and because I want him remembered. Because I made a promise in a hospital room almost six years ago. It was a dark confusing time and I had to be strong for my survivor but I made Willis a promise that he would NEVER be forgotten and I would make sure of that. I don't care what anyone else thinks.

And you know what I've realized who my friends were. Because I have the most amazing friends who like and comment on his pictures and who are totally accepting of me and Walker and Willis. Friends who give me words of encouragement and who say, "We know it's hard." friends who on march 6 wish Walker AND Willis a happy birthday. My dad when asked how many grandkids he has never fails to count Willis. Those are the things that have kept me going in the past six years. That and the sweet little boy who opens the car door for me and who will reach over sometimes out of nowhere and put his hand in mine. And for my other two children who love me and support me.

Seasons mean something different to me since my twins came into my life. In fall I start to remember finding out I was pregnant. In winter, I remember finding out I was having boys and in January I found out about my Willis. In march they were born. And that summer I was a new mother and a grieving mother. And my life changed that year and I was no longer the same person.

I thank God for the memories I had with Willis while I did have him. The sweet seasons of love that will help me remember him forever. Some days I'll always be back in that hospital room holding him for the first time. I'll be on that ultrasound table finding out I'm having twins. I'll be in that car on the way home after finding out my Willis was gone.

Part Two
Double Survivors

Double Survivors

It's easy to look at the double survivors (as a loss parent) and assume they had an easy ride. The truth is, very few families with double TTTS survivors had it "easy". Yes, both babies came home. But almost all of them had to go through the same trials and tribulations during pregnancy, delivered very pre-term, had extensive NICU stays, and had seriousl health issues. Even though they came home with two babies, they are still scarred by TTTS. Some have children with residual health issues. Never the same.

Peyton and Addison
Cameron and Kate
Benjamin and JD
Brady and Brenden
Penn and Cruz
Elena and Diana
Aiden and Jonothan
Landon and Luke
Charlie and Kiera

Adah and Abigail

Grady and Hudson

William and Mason

Cody and Christian

Jordan and Eli

Evelyn and Elizabeth

Peyton and Addison

ReNée Bixler

"... by my God have I leaped over a wall. As for God, His way is perfect."

2 Samuel 22:30-31

I have to admit that I'm a little biased about this story, because Peyton and Addison live nearby and I get to spend time with them every month! Their mama, ReNée, was the first TTTS mother I met and began to bond with, and she and I have become friends. We even have a picture of my Tiny and ReNée's Tiny, Addison at about the same age - they look so similar, even we have a hard time telling them apart! (Weird??) We had the same doctor, our babies were in the same NICU, and we have bonded so much over the past year. We have playdates with our local TTTS Moms (we have a TTTS Survivors Group) and we celebrate our victories and mourn our losses together. ReNée has been a major part of my recovery process!

ReNée is also the creator behind many of the graphics I use on my blog and you can find (and request your own personalized graphics!) at Random ReNée! She has used this experience and combined it with her talents to spread awareness. Not only does she make graphics and awareness banners, she also developed a wonderful educational video for the TTTS Foundation. Her banners provide so much joy and happiness, especially for those of us who have lost one or both of our babies. For example, check out this cute piece she made for me:

So, without further ado, here is Addison and Peyton's story, as told by ReNée!

Peyton and Addison (PandA)

I had 2 miscarriages prior to getting pregnant with my twins. I say that because my Dr. said I could try ONE more time to carry a baby then she wanted to do testing to find out why....3 months later, I found out I was pregnant! I honestly had NO reason to take a pregnancy test the day I did... my husband was out of town for work, I literally was bored and thought why not? Much to my surprise TWO PINK LINES!

I called my husband with plans of being all cute and

telling him, but as soon as he answered I started bawling and said, "I don't want to lose another baby!" to which he replied "Ok???? So, do you not want to try anymore?" and I said, through tears "It's too late!" not quite the cutesy lovey way of telling him, but it really did set the pace for our up and down emotional pregnancy.

I immediately called my doctor and went in a couple of days later.

I had no idea how far along I might be. My best guess was about 5 weeks. So, my Dr. did bloodwork to ensure the baby was progressing (unlike my last two pregnancies) and she called later that day and said "Are you sure you're only 5 weeks?" I nodded. She expressed that the hormone levels seemed to say I was closer to 3 months. Which was not possible since I'd lost a baby then. She wanted me come back in for another blood test the next day. At this point I was already in tears worried that this was BAD. The next day we went in and she drew more blood and she sends me for an ultrasound.... The ultrasound just showed the sack. No "dot" yet.... which was consistent with my thoughts of being about 5 weeks pregnant.

Then my doctor walks in and immediately says "Do twins run in either of you your families?" Honestly, it didn't even phase me or occur to me why she'd ask this, so I said "Yup, both, why?" at this point I look at my husband whose eyes are HUGE and the doctor said, "Well, your hormone levels are REALLY high so either you are much further along than 5 weeks, which we've ruled out or..." and I said innocently and cluelessly "Or what?"

My doctor then said "Well, you are definitely pregnant... It's just a matter of with how many. I'd bet it's three or less."

JAW HIT THE FLOOR! We didn't tell anyone but my parents and best friend that it was likely more than one. They didn't believe it was possible, my mom kept saying "It's not possible" (while giggling!)

Two weeks later at 8-weeks my doctor had me come in for an "official" first visit and did another ultrasound and as soon as the picture appeared, we saw , clearly - TWO DOTS! Both my husband and I were silent except for sniffles! Happiest moment of my life, I'd always wanted twins, and I WAS HAVING TWINS! But that joy changed.... fast.... when the doctor came in.... She looked over the ultrasound and started talking about how it looked like they MIGHT be identical and they MIGHT share a placenta and they MIGHT develop this TTTS thing. But that she wanted me back in 2 weeks to double check once they were more developed.

Two weeks later my husband and I went back in and

she did another ultrasound... Baby B was measuring a few days "behind" Baby A. At this point my doctor earned my HIGHEST respect when she said she really felt it was or would become TTTS and she gave me the limited info she knew, which wasn't much, and was terrifying. She openly and honestly said she did not know much other than, one baby will be smaller and has less fluid and will stop growing and it was VERY fatal and untreatable. But she also wasted no time and made me a referral to the area specialist in TTTS and high risk pregnancies.

My apt was made with the specialist 5-6 weeks later. Between the two appointments, I had to say goodbye to my husband as he deployed for a year tour to Afghanistan. It was the worst day of my life (up until that point) - I was faced with possible TTTS, a pregnancy and being alone. A week later my parents, and I sat at the specialist's office and the ultrasound confirmed the possibility of TTTS.

The doctor came in after the ultrasound to talk to us... and within minutes he had me comforted and scared and happy and worried. I left that office with a heavy yet excited heart. They didn't FOR SURE have TTTS yet, but he really felt they would soon enough. He had me on an every other week appointment routine. And between then and the 12 weeks to follow, every other appointment was up and down. First both babies were ok, then Baby B was getting smaller and smaller, then their fluid levels were equal, then Baby B was less (but not "bad enough" to do anything) it was topsy tervy at best....

Truthfully, I kept ALOT of the ups and downs bottled inside because I didn't want to worry my husband when he was a million miles away fighting a war and had to focus on keeping himself safe.

At 20-weeks a local friend of a friend contacted me and told me her TTTS story and gave me Dr. Delia's contact info and I contacted Dr. Delia via email and he emailed me right away and said BED REST (I'd already put myself on bed rest due to being scared/worried/depressed) but he also told me to drink protein shakes 4-5 a day, sipping them, so I did....

Then at 27weeks + 4 days I went in for my ultrasound, the tech said things looked the same as the previous week. Later that afternoon the doctor's office called. The Dr. looked at the ultrasound and I had to get to the hospital ASAP and to bring enough stuff to stay until the babies were born. It could be any day up to 9 weeks. I called my parents in NC and told them to head down (2.5hrs) and called my Red Cross contact JUST to get a message to my husband to call me because I was at the hospital. And then I had a friend get me to the hospital.

I was at the hospital for 4 hours, checked in, got IV, talked to 100 nurses and THEN a doctor came in and explained that my smaller baby had started to send her blood supply back to the placenta, it was intermittent but it was NOT GOOD if it happened at all. They hooked me up to 100 machines. The doctor explained they'd monitor me overnight and that my doctor would come by the next morning and "decide what we would do".

My husband called from Afghanistan a few hours later and I told him what little I knew. Of course, I downplayed it and acted as casual as possible. The next morning my doctor came in and said the reversal wasn't getting worse but sure wasn't better... And then he said, words I'll never forget.... "If we deliver now you have a good chance, and that's all I can say, a chance, of two healthy babies... if you go to term you will have one live birth and your smaller baby will be still born." My heart sank.... I stared at him and then I said "Are you seriously asking me to decide?" and he said "No, that's the basis for my decision. We need to deliver." This was a Friday. He wanted to deliver Sunday. I agreed.

I called my Red Cross contact again, this time to request my husband come home (which is something they offer in extreme circumstances) to which she told me "I put that request in yesterday when I talked to you,

I just knew it wasn't going to be good." The process had already begun and he'd be home Sunday night, missing the delivery by a few hours.

When I talked to my doctor the next morning he agreed that we could wait until Monday so Josh would be home, but mostly because I'd be 28weeks which would increase their chances of survival even more. We decided to wait until Monday UNLESS the monitoring showed signs of the reversal getting worse or anything changed, in which case I signed/agreed to an emergency C-section. Every time the door to my room opened after that I braced myself that THAT would be the moment!

Sunday night my husband got home and to the hospital at 6pm with the best news he could have brought. His general had discharged him from his deployment. He didn't have to go back! They reassigned him to a job on base locally. To this day, all I can say is, THAT'S GOD, because that is UNHEARD OF in the military. Truthfully though, they did it because they assumed he'd be planning two funerals and grieving and didn't think it would be healthy for him to go back after that. Terrifying to think...

7am on Monday I was being prepped for surgery, with my husband by my side! At 9:18am the doctor held up this baby, this teeny tiny,

Baby A. My Peyton! I have never cried so much in my entire life and I waited I wanted to hear her cry more than anything, but I knew she wouldn't... and then the tears started just in time to hear "Here is baby B" and then they held up Addison. And my heart sank and the tears changed, they changed and my heart broke and I sobbed to my husband "They're never going to make it...."

I NEVER thought such tiny little people would be strong enough. Their faces were 1inch from top to chin. It was the most horrible moment of my life. This was supposed to be a magical amazing moment, giving birth, this was not how I was supposed to feel, this was not how it was supposed to be. THEN, I heard a squeak.... and then another softer squeak and my doctor says "They're crying... both of them... and breathing on their own!!!!!"........silence.... "ReNée that's a really good thing!"

I still didn't know if they'd make it but I had hope, because I heard them cry!!! They brought Addison over to me first for a quick kiss then off to the NICU she went. Then Peyton came by for a quick smooch and away she went to the NICU. My husband went with them.

Once I was back in my room my husband came back and got my dad and grandpa and went to the NICU to show them the babies. (My mom had been in the hall when they pulled then out of the OR so she'd had a peek already and since only 2 guest were allowed in the NICU, she stayed with me.) When my husband came back to show me pictures of my babies he showed me a picture of Addison... wearing his wedding band ON HER ARM.... The most terrifying picture ever! I dropped the camera and was done looking.

Later that night I could be wheeled up to the NICU to see my "Teeny" (Peyton) and my "Tiny" (Addison) as they have been called ever since. They were indeed teeny and tiny and perfect and beautiful!

Our NICU experience only sucked because it was the NICU and our babies were not at home, but I must say aside from that it was a breeze. Addison only had to be ventilated for 18hrs about 2 weeks after birth because she got an infection and couldn't breath and fight it... but other than that.... We had NO issues. They just had to grow. It was frustrating watching the days slowly pass by but we were truly blessed in that there were NO medical issues with either baby.... They just needed time.

At 66 days Peyton came home and it truly broke my heart walking away leaving Addison behind... Thankfully it was only a couple of weeks later and 72 days Addison came home....

Seems like it happened yesterday and it seems a

million years ago, all at the same time.... I never imagined I'd have two survivors. I didn't think I deserved it and after losing 2 babies before birth I had fully resigned myself that God allowed me to have a step daughter (who I ADORE) every other weekend, because that was the only child I'd ever have.... How wrong I was! And how blessed I am.

I am not the type of person to "preach" to anyone I have my faith and I have my beliefs and I hold them close, but I don't force them on others.... But looking at my two miracles I can only say My God is amazing. If I didn't have a strong faith before I sure do now. He has given me everything I ever wanted and more and when I see these two babies I see His grace and His mercy and His love and nothing will ever change that. Bed rest might have helped sustain them. Protein might have evened out their fluid levels from time to time. But I believe God saved my babies and God gave them to me healthy and strong and perfect!

I have recently built up the courage to call the specialists office and ask "what happened" that day at 27 1/2 weeks when I got rushed into the hospital.... According to the nurse (as the doctor no longer practices there), that day when the doctor looked at my ultrasound and turned to her, she said he had a terrible look on his face and said "It happened, they've got TTTS.

We've got to get them out or they're never going to make it." The nurse said they both stood in silence with tears in their eyes and the doctor went on to tell her to call me to the hospital but not to tell me "how bad" because he didn't want to freak me out. She said he told her during this conversation that Peyton had a 10% chance of survival if we didn't deliver and Addison had 0... ZERO %. I am thankful they did not tell me that then, but am glad I know that now. It is extremely humbling. And it further pushes me to press the issue of FREQUENT ULTRASOUNDS for TTTS or potential TTTS pregnancies. Had I not had weekly ultrasound and not had that appointment that day, I would not have my babies now!

My babies are now healthy little girls! Perfectly healthy, perfectly happy! They're right on target developmentally and have only minor medical issues thus far. That amazing in and of itself for any babies born 3 months early and more for TTTS babies! But they are perfect!

Both give us more joy and love then we could ever imagine - our babies - our miracles - our SURVIVORS!

Cameron and Kate

John Dickerson

Marsha Vaughn has become a dear friend of mine, even though we live in two different states. Ironically, we were raised only about 10 miles away from each other, but we did not meet until after our TTTS babies were born. We hit it off and have become dear friends. While we live hours apart now, we make an effort to see each other whenever we can. I'm so glad her husband decided to share their story for the book.

Cameron and Kate

SO here we were.... Walking into the doctor for our first ultrasound. Full of hope, ambition, nerves etc. that come with finding out about your new child to be. It was my second, but Marsha's first... and I guess in recollection at that point I was the calmer one.

We had the discussions – do we want to know the sex? What are some potential names? But we both knew on the first visual, all we wanted and could expect was a confirmation of life... and boy did we.

We were escorted in, momma to be was prepped, and I was sitting off on the side. The tech introduced us to her trainee and told us to be comfortable... And away we went.

Initially there was medical language between them, and general conversations towards us about finding and seeing the heartbeat, and the wand kept moving... until there became looks back and forth, and more comments like, "You see that?" "You hear that?" – all the while pretty much stopping the conversation direction towards us.

At one point, I remember speaking aloud... "You see what? What do you hear" – the look on Marsha's face and the pit of my stomach were now on high alert... and the response I received was, "Well, we see two". I quickly responded, " You see two what"? "Two heartbeats"... and it still didn't register. I don't think to Marsha either until what was probably about 30 seconds later, but felt like an eternity, "You have twins"....

Marsha and I both were in shock and awe... twins? really? We were unprepared for that answer... in fact after some small chat, I don't believe I said two words for the next 3-4 hours.

Fast forward to a new set of doctors, at ROC in Jacksonville. Multiple and high risk specialists. A whole new world of guidelines, and things to be mindful of, and yes. TTTS was mentioned. Around 11 weeks along, it was confirmed identical as only one placenta detected, and were "Mono-Di". The risk for TTTS was / seemed no higher than any other risk we were informed of, and we were still trying to take it all in.

That seemed life for the next few weeks. I think still in awe, and awash with double everything... and back to the original discussions... names, do we want to know the sex, how would we fit an instant double addition in the home... double strollers, diapers, clothes and so on. What and when and how would we tell the family?

At 16 / 5 – Marsha went to the doctor and the next thing I know I am getting a call from her, she was disturbed, and needed to conference me in with the doctor. Ok – deep breath – fill me in. TTTS had developed and we needed to get to see a specialist immediately. The doctor of recommendation was Dr. Ruben Quintero – in Miami. A few calls between the docs – and we left for home to pack some bags and leave early in the morning to drive. We made arrangements for our son, animals, and a sleepless night, and we were off.

It was a quiet ride at times, and some comforting time for both of us to try to grasp what was happening... and what we knew for sure, it was not good.

Dr. Quintero's staff was incredible and comforting, warm and described what was next. A 4-hour 3D ultrasound to see the degree that umbilical cords had fused – and a consultation about our options. We had been told a few of these already to be able to prepare ourselves and didn't like potentially having to "choose" something... looking back and knowing what I know now, I feel incredibly lucky to have had the chance at a choice as many have not.

Dr. Quintero greeted us, made some small chat and quickly got down to business. He thought he could do the surgery, and was willing to proceed. It was a laser ablation, intrusive, but it was an option.

Termination was an option. Doing nothing was an option. We would have a fatal pregnancy if we did not take some sort of option. We could terminate one, to give the other a better chance... my brain is warping... which one? Really? We sat and chatted and quickly agreed there is only one option, the one Dr. Quintero initially said – trust him to do the surgery and give both of them a chance. Albeit a smaller chance than 1, a better chance than none.

He severed 19 veins – 8 major and 11 minor. He felt he got it all... Marsha did great, and now we wait. We wait for a sign from them that the surgery had its initial effect, and improvement evident. It was.

10 weeks later, and home, another turn... Marsha needed bedrest. And immediate. Things were again volatile, and the goal line was 34-0... to be in field goal range. Without significant reduction in movement that only the bed rest could provide, things were not going to improve and I had to guarantee it could happen at home. New bed, reading material, adjustment of TV location and we tried to settle in. We had 8 weeks and our anxiety was growing.

Marsha was on 3x per week ultrasounds, and each one showed progress, so hope continued. At 34-0, we were in the ROC office and it was noticed her placenta was breaking down... with no notice again, we were headed to surgery for our twins' arrival. Wow – it's here, and we still aren't prepared. Marsha was prepped, sent in and I joined her. Kate came first – 4.6lbs. swept away by the NICU staff. Camden, recipient, came next at 3.1lbs and gone even faster. I rushed in for an update... Marsha was taken to recovery, my nerves were a wreck.

We were updated they were stable, small, premature and needed time. Camden was so very tiny compared to our older son... my wedding ring fit over her hand like a bracelet. Talk about perspective.

We welcomed our girls in, and knew a long journey ahead. The girls came home within 2-3 weeks and every checkup we waited with baited breath on how they were doing... each one came with blessed news. It wasn't until their 1 year checkup that I felt the constant pull of fear leave me. I now felt I could trust the trend of progress.

Our girls are our miracles. Full of life, minimal if any repercussions, except for maybe some attitude – and for their journey I always try to be mindful and count is as another blessing.

My faith was tested, both personally and spiritually... I have learned not to take so much for granted, nor seriously. I would gladly trade some attitude, some standing their ground on cleaning up after themselves, some pickiness on eating for not having this chance at all.

I understand I had choices many do not. I understand I had an outcome many do not. I cannot imagine the varying degree of emotions others have had to face considering their own circumstances. My heart absolutely extends out to all that have faced the tests with differed outcomes. I don't feel guilty for my miracles and I know lots who do, and have read many stories about lots who feel I should. I am sorry I can't. I count every day, feel only lucky, the luckiest, this is / was beyond any conceivable lottery winning possible. And I will educate my daughters not to take for granted anything...

My partner and life's journey best friend Marsha deserves all my gratitude and love. This test pushed our limits, and to some degree continues to do so. And I can only say I wouldn't trade it for any alternative.

Benjamin and JD

Shasta Brown

Shasta's TTTS experience with her twin sons Benjamin and JD is both happy and sad. Thankfully Shasta has double survivors, but that does not mean it was an easy journey. Sadly, her friend was also pregnant with identical twins, but lost both of hers due to TTTS at 19 weeks. Similar to me, Shasta already had two kids and decided to have another baby and were surprised to find out we had 2 in there! I guess you never know when you may be blessed with a bonus baby.

Benjamin and JD

I already had 2 older girls when we decided to try for 1 more baby. We figured after 1 more, we would be done. I also knew that my previous 2 pregnancies had ended horribly and a little on the early side. The early part wouldn't have been an issue, but with my oldest I had a rare side effect because of the epidural I had to get to lower my blood pressure. Well, she was born dead (and was revived after-I'm not sure how long it took). So, she was in the NICU for a little while because of that. I knew I ended up with pre-eclampsia but also every doctor kept telling me that most women get that and usually it doesn't repeat.

Since I put a 3-year gap between all of my pregnancies, I was told to go ahead and try for the 3rd. So, we did.

At the same time, a friend of mine named Jenny, was just finding out she was pregnant. I was thrilled for her. We share something in common with how horrid our pregnancies are-we both get very severe hyperemesis. It's where you throw up anything and everything and you can't keep it down. It feels involuntary and I absolutely hate it. Unfortunately, this makes it extremely hard to want any other pregnancies because of how miserable and sick we are during them. So, when she was about 6 or 7 weeks, she found out she was having identical twins. I was so excited for her. She was miserable though. I thought we were still trying to get pregnant, but little did I know-I was already pregnant as well!!!

I woke up after a random dream one night. In my

dream, I walked into the bathroom, took out the pregnancy test, and it immediately turned positive-there was no waiting period. Well, after I woke up, I walked into the bathroom, found the pregnancy test in the exact place I dreamed it was and took the test. By the time I put the test on the counter-it was very positive-there was no waiting.

That never happened with me before. I knew something was up. About 3 weeks later, I knew something was up-I had to get my pregnancy jeans out. I was only like 6 weeks!!! I ended up having an ultrasound at 8 weeks because I had been to the ER to get re-hydrated at least 4 times by then. I was miserable as well.

At that ultrasound-the tech asked, "did you do IVF?" Now I knew she wasn't really asking me how I became pregnant, rather she was telling me, I was having multiples. My heart stopped when I asked how many were there and she said she was counting!!! Oh my goodness!!!

At the end of the ultrasound I was told I was having identical twins and that there was a rare disease called TTTS that I should look out for. What?? How do I look out for it? He also told me that it wasn't a big deal and that nothing will most likely happen. Whew-ok, well if he wasn't worried then neither was I.

Jenny and I continued to hang out-she was 4 weeks ahead and our miserable selves kept us entertained. I would go over there with my then 3 year girl and her 3 year old daughter would play and drive us nuts while we laid on the couches and watched TV together. Misery loves company, right? One day, Jenny called me and told me she was in labor-she was 19 weeks. We both laughed because I told her how miserable it would be to hang out in the hospital for the rest of her pregnancy. She went for an ultrasound and I called her back because it was taking too long. She was crying and very upset.

They told her that her boys had stage 5 TTTS and there was nothing that could be done. She had to deliver them. I started crying with her. I didn't know what else to do. I stayed on the phone for a few more minutes and then I told her I would call her back. I got out of bed-it was about 4:30 pm-I was deathly sick that day. It hurt to move. I was so dehydrated.

I googled ways to help a grieving mother. I spent 20 minutes trying to find a good way to help her. I called her back and told her I was bringing over my camera (that I had just bought from her) and I told her that she needed to take pics. I said to her that I read online that it helps to have pics because she won't have anything else from this pregnancy. She was very happy about that. She knew I was sick and didn't want to ask. I hurried it over to the hospital and went to see her. We just sat there and cried together for a few minutes.

There was nothing that could be said. She asked me if I thought her boys would be born alive. She wanted more than anything to see them alive. I looked at her and with tears in my eyes I told her I thought they would be. Her boys were born alive just a few hours later. Jax and Rook lived for a few hours. She took lots of pictures and I've seen a few of them since then.

I called my OB about 3 days later and demanded to see a high-risk doctor. It took 3 days because every time I thought of doing anything I just sat and cried. During those 3 days I fielded the questions from people in our church on how to help. Everyone called me and asked me what to do and I did it. I needed to. I was so sad but I helped.

2 weeks later I went into the high-risk doc and they told me I had stage 3 TTTS. I went to Baltimore a few hours away to Dr. Baschat and I spent another 3 hours trying to figure out how advanced I was. I had a very aggressive stage 3. Dr. Baschat is awesome, by the way. He gave me 3 options. He said I could have an abortion (although he said he wouldn't be doing that at his office-he didn't believe in it), I could wait and see or I could try the surgery.

My stomach turned at the thought of ending the pregnancy-even though I was beyond miserably sick (I was throwing up bile). But, I still couldn't end it. I knew what waiting would give me.

Surgery it was. Surgery was set for the next morning. I went back home to Virginia (a 1.5 hour drive without traffic). My husband and I drove back to Baltimore the next morning. A few hours later I had the surgery. By then, I had stage 4 TTTS. I knew death was stage 5. They even asked if they should do the surgery because I was so advanced and with a 10% chance of getting 1 baby-would it be worth it??

I don't blame them for asking-honestly, the deck was stacked against us. We all decided that I was already there and prepped and if I had to be on Magnesium I better have something done. Well, the next morning, things were just ok. Nothing improved, but the boys were alive. I stayed in Baltimore for the weekend. I went back with news that the boys were alive, but that's about it.

So, for the next 6 weeks I was in Dr. Baschat's care and I drove up there every Tuesday. That was the longest drive ever, and I repeated it for 6 weeks. For the first few weeks-not much was improving. Honestly, I am not sure how they were alive. JD (donor) barely had amniotic fluid but there was more than before the surgery. My Benjamin (recipient) still had an enlarged heart and fluid around it. After the 3rd week of nothing really improving-I honestly sat there and thought "if these babies are born with these problems, what have I done?" I was scared and I was sad-did I really doom my boys to a life of extreme health problems??

Well, I went for the 4th and 5th time. Still things were the same. I hated that drive more than anything. Traffic around DC is horrid and did nothing for my mood. But, I was still pregnant while Jenny wasn't so I decided that I would take on whatever happened. I was grateful and that was that.

On week 6, I show up for my ultrasound and in the middle of it Dr. Baschat looked at me and said, "I can't believe it!!! The TTTS has been completely reversed. Your boys are perfectly fine!!" I said what? How can that be? I sat there for about another hour while he checked everything over and over again. He couldn't believe it. At that appointment, I felt hope. At that appointment, I was released from his care and back to the Perinatologist in Virginia. I was 20 weeks then.

At 23 weeks, there was evidence of reverse flow. I was admitted into the hospital that day. I sat in the hospital for 4 weeks during the swine flu scare. My older girls couldn't see me except for on Sundays. Once a week, I could see them. I didn't get many visitors. When I was 24 weeks, Jenny called me and asked how she could help us out. I was shocked. Up until then-she kept her distance. She was battling extreme depression and couldn't even bear to look at me. So... imagine my surprise when she called me. I asked why she wanted to help. She said, "I am praying your boys aren't born now. I don't want you to lose your boys as well. I am praying they will live." I was stunned into silence. She cared. She maintained her distance, but she honestly cared. She didn't want me to go through a funeral like she did. She cared. My hope was straight back up in the sky. She watched my 3-year-old girl until my husband's mom could get there a week later.

At 27 weeks 5 days, I had my boys. It was an emergency C-section and I was put under. I kept asking if the boys were alive when I woke up. I just needed to be reassured. I couldn't go see them.

A friend of mine who worked in the NICU came down and told us about our boys though. He was their doctor for the first little while. The boys had heart surgery to close their PDA but that was really it. The donor, (JD), his lungs were shot. He was born at 27 weeks and change, but we were told his lungs were that of a 24-weeker because of how severe the TTTS was.

He struggled. He turned blue several times and when I was there. I remember the first time-he turned blue and his numbers dropped to 0. My husband and I looked at each other and just stared at each other. There was nothing we could do but watch the docs and nurses bring him back to us.

That's all we did with him for 8 long weeks. We sat and watched. We were too afraid to touch him-when we did, he didn't like it and would de-sat big time. Benjamin didn't have such a hard time. He let me cuddle with him after 2 or 3 weeks. I demanded Kangaroo Care with him. My heart needed to heal and I believe he helped with that. After 3 and 3.5 months-I brought them home.

I was on my own because my husband used all of his time because of everything that had happened. I was exhausted and was still battling myself.

I felt guilty, I felt I couldn't be too happy because it would upset my friend. I know that's not what she would have wanted, but it's how I felt. And, at the time, I was only a member of another TTTS group and I was always told that I can't feel sad because they are living.

I was told how dare I be sad at all-I should be grateful.

I was told very cruel things by people. And I let it get to me.

I fought myself for so long. My boys will be 3 very soon and every day I look at them and smile. Every day I see the smiles of those who can't be here as well. I'm reminded of everything we went through to get them here.

Before I moved away from the DC area, Jenny was expecting her 3rd son. She was in the hospital and her mom was staying and watching her daughter. Her mom said, "I am so glad you 2 are still friends. I know she tried her hardest to push you away and anyone else would have gone away. You didn't give up on her. She told me the other day how grateful she was you still talked to her. I know you went through a lot as well to get your twins here. She needed to see that so you two could stay friends. She needed to see how hard it really is, she needed to know you fought hard. She loves you as a friend, more than you will ever know. I will miss you and she will miss you so much. Thank you for not giving up on her."

Brady and Brenden

Brandi McMahan

Brady and Brenden are two more miracle babies, thankfully both with us, but it was a difficult journey none the less! Their mother Brandi also had an anterior placenta and was able to have the laser ablation surgery. I share that because MY doctor told me I was ineligible for surgery due to an anterior placenta. So, I reiterate - make sure you get in touch with a TTTS expert if you or someone you know is diagnosed with TTTS! Because not all OBs (and even the MFMs) are knowledgeable on the subject.

Brady and Brenden

Ben and I found out on January 6, 2011 that we were expecting our 1st child. My pregnancy was confirmed on January 14, 2011 and an ultrasound was scheduled for the 25th in order to determine how far along my pregnancy was. At that ultrasound, we found out that we were not only about 6 weeks and that our due date was September 18, 2011 but that we were also expecting twins. Shocked doesn't even begin to describe the way we felt!! Although we were shocked and scared we were overjoyed that God had picked us to be the parents of twins!! We felt blessed beyond words once the shock wore off of course!!

On March 16th, I had to see a high-risk doctor for the 1st time. We were assured the only reason we had to see this doctor was because we were having twins and a multiple pregnancy is automatically high risk. At that appointment, we got to see our tiny babies on another ultrasound and we found out that they were identical and sharing a placenta. Dr. Bansal mentioned the possibility of something called TTTS and told us it was only a 15% chance of our babies getting it so we weren't too worried and didn't really share to much about TTTS with our families. We figured since the chance was so low that we shouldn't stress over it at this point.

A few weeks later, on April 13th I had another ultrasound. Ben and my mom went to the appointment with me because it was the day we were going to find out if our babies would be girls or boys. I knew I would love them either way but I hoped and prayed with every ounce of my being that I would hear the word BOYS!! The ultrasound tech began the exam and within a few minutes she looked at Ben and said "do you see that?" And we knew what that meant!! She said "Baby A is a boy and even though Baby B is being shy we know he's a boy too!" I immediately began to think of how excited my daddy would be and how I was going to tell everyone! I could barely contain my excitement!

Brady and Brenden are the 1st boys in my family in a LONG time! When they were born it was 24 years on my dad's side since there had been a boy and 47 years (I think) on my mom's. I just couldn't help but feel even more blessed at that moment. Through all the excitement I wiped a tear from my eye thinking how happy my Papa would be to have twin great grandsons and my heart was saddened that he would never know them and they would never know him as he passed in 2007. But I knew they had a guardian angel watching over them.

A little bit after we found out they were boys the ultrasound tech told us she was done and had to go get the doctor. We thought nothing about this because at our 1st appointment he came in and looked at the boys as well. When Dr. B came in he had a distressed look on his face and he looked even more worried the longer he looked at the boys on the ultrasound. After he was done he told me that we were dealing with TTTS. He informed us that it was a severe case as our Baby B didn't have a visible bladder. He explained that basically our Baby B who was the donor was giving all the nutrients, blood flow and amniotic fluid to our Baby A who is called the recipient. The boys didn't have names at this point.

So, he went through the options for treatment with us. He explained that they do a procedure called amnioreduction which removes the excess fluid from the recipient and would increase his chance of survival, however since our donor was so "sick" it would more than likely not do much to help him. He also told us that we could terminate our donor in order to save our recipient or terminate the entire pregnancy. He wasn't for termination but he had to offer it to us.

He said we could do nothing and let nature run its course and face an almost 99% chance of miscarriage of both babies. And last he told us about a laser surgery that could reverse the TTTS is successful and increase the survival of both babies. As we sat in his office that day in tears and complete fear of what would happen to our babies we knew that we had to fight for them.

In our opinion terminating one or both was giving up on the fight. We knew that no matter what that wasn't an option for us and the only option we could choose was the laser surgery. It was the only option that could give BOTH of our babies a chance at the life they deserved and we wanted them to have. We told him that our decision was the laser surgery. He explained that no one in the Atlanta area did the surgery and we would have to travel to Cincinnati Ohio to have the procedure done. At that moment in my life I had NO IDEA where Cincinnati was, how long it would take us to get there, and how we would get there at a moment's notice as we hadn't been planning to take a trip.

On Sunday April 17th, we got up early to head to Cincinnati. We drove because my doctor didn't want the added stress of the airport and a plane ride on me since I had never flown before. We had to stop every hour in order for me to empty my bladder regardless if I felt the need to or not. By doing this it helped keep pressure off my uterus and cervix to help keep me from contracting.

On Monday the 18th I went to Cincinnati Children's Hospital in order to have testing done. It was a long day! I had to have an EKG, MRI (for the babies) Echo (on the babies) blood work and we had to have a meeting with the doctors to make sure I still qualified for the surgery. They told me I was a stage 3c at this point and needed to do the surgery as soon as possible. However, I couldn't have it until Thursday because I had just had a cerclage. I returned to the hospital on Thursday April 21st at 18w3d for the surgery to save my boys. I was prepped for the surgery and went in as bravely as possible by myself to have the procedure done.

We were told the surgery could take anywhere from 1-3 hours. My mom, dad and Ben waited for information from the doctors in the waiting area. The surgery went much faster than expected. the doctor's thought it would be difficult because I had an anterior placenta which can complicate the surgery and getting the laser where it needed to be to laser the connections. Brady and Brenden had 10 connections that were lasered and they poked a tiny hole in the membrane that separated them to help the amniotic fluid to even out between the boys. My family was terrified when the doctor came out to tell them the news so soon but they were quickly calmed when the doctor told them the surgery went as well as it could have and that I and both babies were doing fine at that point.

Then the wait began. All we could do was wait until the next morning to see if both boys survived the surgery. I got good during this time in my life at hiding my fear and trying to stay strong and positive. I didn't sleep much that night. I was so concerned with making sure I could feel movement in my tummy. I laid there in that hospital bed watching my husband sleep wondering if we would leave that hospital as a family of 4 like we came, a family of 3 or my biggest fear, leaving as a family of 2. That was the longest 24 hours of my life.

The next morning the nurses came in, put me in a wheel chair and wheeled me to the ultrasound room. The tech began the scan and I very impatiently waited to see and hear heart beats. I was relieved when she said "there is baby a" and I cried tears of joy when she said "and there is baby b" WE DID IT!! We still had two strong heart beats!!

But my days in Cincinnati weren't over. I was sent back to the Ronald McDonald House on bed rest until the following Tuesday. On Tuesday April 26th, we went back to the hospital for another follow up. We had several tests that day as well. And we still had TWO heart beats.

At this point my fear was starting to ease. We were cleared to head back home the next day.

Upon arriving home I was on strict bed rest, which I often referred to as "House Arrest." Just imagine for a minute being put on bed rest when you weren't even 1/2 way through a pregnancy. Imagine Laying in the bed or on the couch day in and day out wondering if your babies were still alive. Many people think that the surgery fixed the TTTS and my worries were over. That is so far from true. I had to have an ultrasound weekly to make sure they were still ok.

On June 16th, I got up to get ready for my every Thursday doctor appointment and found that I was bleeding. I yelled for my mom and we immediately went to the doctor. I was admitted into the hospital that day for preterm labor. They started magnesium sulfate to stop the contractions and labor. I was informed that I would be there until I delivered the boys, didn't matter if it was that day, the next week or two months from then. I hated the thought of being in the hospital that long but I was willing to do whatever was best for my boys and I knew that the hospital was the best place to be.

That night was rough. Magnesium is horrible, it made me sick and I felt like I was on fire. It was the middle of June and people were wearing coats in the room with me because I had it so cold so I could be comfortable and I was still hot!! The Mag worked!! My labor stopped and I was taken off the IVs. I felt wonderful. The boys were being monitored around the clock. I could hear them move and hear their hearts beating. For the first time since my TTTS diagnosis I knew they were ok and I could sleep without fear.

Unfortunately, the Mag only held off my labor about 36-48 hours and it was coming back. This time I felt the pain and contractions a lot stronger. They hooked the I with the Mag back up and started the process over. It took a little longer for the pain to stop this time but in time, it did. I felt like a million bucks again.

I began having pain again that night and yep! You guessed it here comes the lovely Mag and IVs again. Ben was hesitant to leave since I was having pain but once again I assured him I was fine and my mom was there. So, he left. I was in a lot of pain that night and the pain meds they were giving me wasn't helping. Ben called me at 5:30am to make sure I was ok and if he needed to come to the hospital or if he should head to work. I told him I had a painful, sleepless night but I thought I was ok and sent him to work. It was about 8am when I decided something wasn't right and had my mom tell the nurse to get my doctor.

The doctor sent in a midwife who checked me and informed us I was already an 8, he told my mom she'd better get my husband on the phone and get him there quickly. My mom frantically called him and everyone else. He got there just as they were taking me to the OR, he changed and ran in to be with me!

They were born 6/24/11 at 27 weeks. Brady Michael was born at 9:57am at 2 lb 2 oz and Brenden Ray at 10:04 weighing 2lbs. Both were a tiny 13 3/4 inches.

The boys spent three months in the NICU before they

could come home on 9/24/11.

Although I knew we were being discharged, I had the urge to RUN out of the NICU, like I was kidnapping my own babies. I will admit, that thought crossed my mind a few times during their stay. FINALLY after 92 long days we were leaving the hospital the way we should be leaving....as a family of FOUR!

Brady and Brenden are my everything. They are healthy boys that are full of life and energy and into everything and I wouldn't have it any other way. Sometimes I catch myself staring at them while they play together and it brings all the memories of my pregnancy and NICU back to me. It reminds me how lucky and blessed they are to have each other and how blessed I am to have them. I am reminded of my fight and the fact I was told IF they survived they would more than likely have lifelong disabilities and once again I think "WE BEAT YOU TTTS, TAKE THAT!"

My boys are healthy but there are many moms that went through what I did that didn't get my happy ending. Babies lose their lives every day to this evil thing called TTTS, with every new death I hear of and every family that has been torn apart and may never feel complete my heart breaks, I cry for them and I grab my boys and hold them even tighter. For this reason, my fight with TTTS will never end. Until there is a cure for

TTTS I will FIGHT TTTS forever!!

Penn and Cruz

Shann Soiney

It's always strange reading these stories because sometimes they can be so similar. When Shann describes her experience of being on continuous monitoring in the hospital, and how once a nurse had to sit with her for three hours while trying to find the heartbeats... that happened to me several times as well. Even when TTTS stories do not have the same outcome, they have many of the same "middle" parts.

Penn and Cruz

I've been wanting to tell the story of my pregnancy for some time now. Not only is it hard to find time, but anytime I do have, I try to grab a nap. Raising 3 kids under 3 is hard! Plus, I don't know that I'm ready to relive all the emotions of my pregnancy. It was really one of the hardest things I've had to go through in my life.

While the 3 months in the NICU were extremely difficult, I had wonderful nurses and doctors to help in the twins' care. When I was pregnant, I felt like I was the only one responsible for them. I know the doctors were monitoring me and my family helped me make decisions, but ultimately, the babies were in my body and it felt like every decision I made could have been life or death for one or both of the babies. It was a really heavy emotional time for me.

So, I am going to tell a shorter version of my pregnancy, and not go week by week, as I hope to eventually do. Someday I will have the strength to share everything, but for now, here are the basics.

Last fall, I was having some health issues having to do with my bladder and kidneys. The issues have since resolved themselves, but at the time it was very stressful going through a bunch of tests and constantly taking antibiotics. I saw countless doctors and specialist and no one could figure out exactly why I kept getting infections. Then, at the beginning of December, I found out I was pregnant. I got extreme morning (rather all day) sickness, and had to leave my job. I didn't tell anyone I was pregnant because I am very superstitious about not telling anyone until after the first trimester is over. Well, we planned to tell everyone after our 12-week ultrasound, but we got bad news. The nuchal fold on one of the babies (yes I said one of the babies, we found out it was twins...that was awesome news!) was enlarged.

Because they were identical and sharing a placenta, this enlargement could have indicated a chromosomal abnormality in both babies. We were rushed to Froedert for a CVS (where they take a needle and get a sample from the placenta) to find out what we were dealing with. After almost 2 weeks, we got the call that everything was ok and breathed a huge sigh of relief.

Unfortunately, this was only the beginning. At the next ultrasound, it was discovered the babies were over 20% discordant in size. When twins share a placenta, this is indicative of either unequal placental share or TTTS (twin to twin transfusion syndrome) Both are very dangerous, and the survival rates of both babies are not very encouraging. Basically, when it is unequal placental share, one baby will eventually run out of placenta, and thus nutrients, and have to be delivered because there is no treatment. Babies are only considered viable at 24 weeks, and a full-term pregnancy is 40 weeks. In TTTS, because of the shared connections in the placenta, one baby takes the nutrients from the other, and therefore the blood. One baby's heart will then have to work very hard to pump all the extra blood and the other will start losing functions of its organs, starting with its bladder.

There is a laser surgery that can be performed for TTTS, but you must meet certain criteria, such as large enough amounts of amniotic fluid, and it is still very dangerous to the babies. The goal of the surgery is to separate the connection between the babies because if one should pass, the other one would get a sudden rush of blood, which can result in brain damage or death. So, throughout my entire pregnancy, I was monitored for either/both of these conditions. I had weekly, sometimes bi-weekly ultrasounds. I also changed my care from the original Maternal Fetal Specialist at Waukesha to a specialist at St. Joe's.

Dr. Julian De Lia was the pioneer of TTTS laser surgery, and we are lucky enough to have him in Milwaukee. He is truly an amazing man, coming to every single ultrasound, even though he was technically on sabbatical. Not only did I make the decision to be in his care because of his expertise, but because the other doctor told me I should consider cord ligation. Cord ligation is basically clamping the cord of the smaller baby to save the bigger baby. He did not believe my smaller baby would make it to viability, and even if he did, he didn't believe he would be big enough to save, which he considered 500 grams, or a little over a pound.

I couldn't bring myself to pick to save one baby over the other, so I had to find a doctor that would support my decision. Dr. De Lia was that doctor. Every week, from week 16 of my pregnancy, I would head to St. Joe's for an ultrasound. This was the only place I would go, as I was on bed rest. I also had to force myself to drink three high protein Ensure shakes a day, plus try to get as much protein from other foods as possible. I was still nauseous, and food had absolutely no appeal, but I ate for my babies. It was one of the only things I could do. I even put an Ensure in a cooler in the bathroom, so every time I got up to pee, I would sip some of it.

Bed rest was sheer torture. I would lay on the couch at my Mom's house unable to take care of my other child, Bex. I was completely dependent on my parents and my husband. I felt like such a burden. I also was emotionally drained. Since I couldn't really do anything but watch TV or go on the computer, I sat all day worrying about my babies and how this was affecting everyone in my life. It was taking an emotional toll on everyone I loved. It's hard to be responsible for the pain you see in your loved one's faces. My blood pressure was so high at the beginning of each visit from my stress level that they would have to retake it after the scan. The ultrasounds looked to see what the fluid difference was between the babies, the weight difference, and they also looked at how the blood was flowing from the placenta. They needed to make sure both babies were growing and that there was some good blood flow. The smaller baby had a bad cord insertion, so he did not receive as many nutrients and therefore grew at a much slower rate. The blood did not always flow forward, but it would stop, and sometimes reverse, which they call absent end diastolic flow and intermittent reverse flow.

They also guessed that since my fluids were in the very ends of the normal range, there was a mild transfusion and that they had a very unequal share of the placenta. So my babies were fighting both conditions, TTTS and SIUGR. By week 21, I could start to feel them moving around. In some ways, it was good, in some ways it was terrifying. I was always afraid I could only feel one baby moving, and that we would show up at the next ultrasound to only one heartbeat.

By some miracle, I made it to 24 weeks. At that appointment, I asked the doctor if I should stay in the hospital for constant monitoring. He hesitated, but then agreed. Even though I had been on bed rest at home, the hospital was a whole new level of torture. I missed my 2-year-old terribly and also felt so guilty for everyone else having to take care of him. I had never been away from my son for even a night before this experience. In addition to that, the more pressing concern was for the babies. They would hook up monitors to find the heartbeats three times a day at the beginning. Because the babies were so small, it was hard to find them, and even once they did, they rarely stayed still. One night a nurse sat pressing the monitors on my belly for over three hours. Eventually, they went to constant monitoring, which was so uncomfortable, but I wanted to do whatever I could to save both my babies.

On the morning of Friday, May 4th, around 5:45, I was alone in my room. I started to drift to sleep, but I heard the slow beeping of the monitor. Even though the monitor also monitored my heart, I knew it was too slow to be me. I called the nurses, and sure enough, baby A's heart was decelerating. It had been beating very slowly for 5 minutes, indicating he was in distress. Three nurses rushed in, followed by the Doctor on call. They turned me to my side and gave me oxygen. The Doctor brought the ultrasound machine and asked me, "Are you ok with letting me take the babies out if I see them in distress?" I, of course, agreed to do what was best for them. He looked quickly at the ultrasound and shouted to book the Operating Room.

I was extremely frightened. I'd never had major surgery before, and had a natural birth with Bex. I wanted to call my husband and mom, but there was not time. They rushed me into the room, took off my pants and rolled me onto the table. They inserted a catheter, and then the anesthesiologist came over. I reminded the nurse to tell everyone that the babies shared a placenta, so they may need blood volume after delivery. Dr. DeLia, my doctor, had reminded me to do that because in this kind of pregnancy complications can arise at the last minute. After the nurse told everyone, I remember the anesthesiologist telling everyone to be quiet because I wasn't out yet.

I remember praying that I wouldn't feel them cut me open and that my babies would both be alive. The next thing I remember is coughing and being rolled into the recovery room. My mom was there and then Andy was there shortly. The nurse told me both babies were ok and in the NICU. After a few minutes, they were able to roll me into the NICU to see them. I remember my mom being teary eyed and saying how perfect they were. My dad and brother also came and got to see the boys. I just felt a great relief that they were both ok and that the pregnancy was finally over.

My twin boys were born by emergency C-section at 9:49am on Friday, May 4th, 2012. At just 25 weeks and 5 days, Baby A weighed 1lb and 7.5oz and Baby B weighed 2lbs and 2oz. After examination of the placenta, it was found that there were 4 connections between the babies. Baby B had about 10% of the placenta, and his cord was hanging out into the membrane, not connected directly to the placenta. We were lucky we delivered when we did. My boys spent 91 and 93 days in the NICU and went through many complications, but I am happy to say they are now home and doing well. They are currently 18 months and weigh over 21 and 26lbs.

Elena and Diana

Laura DeLancy

Elena and Diana's story

Three years ago in March I found out that I was pregnant, it was shocking as it was not planned at all, we had 3 children already, had discussed having 4 but didn't think it would happen so soon with our youngest being 6 mo. old at the time.

I remember how shocked I was because we had been taking every precaution and I was also breastfeeding the youngest. I found out on a Saturday and then took another test the following Tuesday when the 2nd test was positive I called my OBGYN for an appointment. The appointment was scheduled for April 22nd almost 4 weeks away, I didn't want to wait that long, but they said i needed to be at least 6 weeks along to get a good ultrasound reading.

Time drug on, but eventually April 22nd arrived and I was nervous, they took me back to ultrasound and asked me to take a pregnancy test just to be sure, then they proceeded with the ultrasound. All the sudden I heard "there are 2 in there"!

I said What! as I stared at the screen in utter amazement, my mom was with me and was also very shocked. My husband and I wanted 4 kids and yet now we would have 5, it would be a lot of work but I knew we could do it.

At the time of the ultrasound I was actually 9 weeks pregnant, little did I know that in 9 more weeks things would change. When i got home and told my husband he was just as shocked as I was, it was then that we started telling people that we were having identical twins. Life was good and we were thrilled.

9 weeks later at a routine ultrasound the 4th ultrasound of the pregnancy my OB said he saw a size difference between the girls and said that he was concerned that it might be TTTS and wanted me to see a Perinatologist about this. So, he sent me to Charleston, WV to see Dr. B at CAMC women's and Children's hospital.

Dr. B. did a very lengthy ultrasound where they did several measurements and other readings, then they told me that the twins were girls. After the ultrasound, they took me to a consultation room where it seemed I waited forever until Dr. B came in and told me that the girls had what is called TTTS or Twin to Twin Transfusion Syndrome. He explained that baby A Elena was the recipient because she was the bigger of the 2, and baby B Diana was the donor and was giving her sister most of her blood and nutrients. He said that the best thing to do would be to go to the Fetal Care Center of Cincinnati to have a procedure known as Laser Ablation done, where they would go in and cauterize the 4 blood vessels that were causing Elena to receive the extra blood and nutrients, that he was hopeful that the procedure would work.

In attempt to be closer to home and to possibly stay with family I did some research to find another possible location to have the procedure done and Dr. E in Pittsburgh popped up. At the time I was told by his staff that he had done the procedure while supervised but had never done it solo. This concerned me a lot and Mary from the TTTS Foundation talked to me and calmed me down she assured me that the better doctors were in Cincinnati and although the doctor in Pittsburgh was capable he was not that experienced.

I went to see Dr. E in Pittsburgh and after a 3 hour ultrasound he told me that I had 5 options, 1. Do nothing and let them die, 2 save the bigger one to save the smaller one, 3 terminate the entire pregnancy because I already had 3 healthy children at home, 4 Amnio Reduction would not likely help and because of my weight I was not a good candidate for the surgery.

I decided at that point that i would go to Cincinnati, the next morning after I had gotten home from Pittsburgh, Dr. E called to say that he had scheduled an Amnio Reduction with Dr. B in Charleston and that i would need to go to Cincinnati to have the surgery done later that week. The Amnio reduction took place on July 2nd I remember it well it was a Friday. The following Tuesday I was scheduled for the surgery under the very capable hands of Dr. L and his team at the Fetal Care Center of Cincinnati.

After a lot of tests, they told me that the girls were in stage 4 and we had to act almost immediately and scheduled me for surgery the next day. they had told me that when they did the MRI that it showed that Elena had 90% of the placenta and that Diana only had 10% of the placenta and had fluid on her brain.

The next day the surgery went as planned and they were very hopeful that things would be better, they told me that after the surgery that if Diana was going to make it she was going to have to fight. The next morning they did an ultrasound and sent me to my hotel room for the week until I would have to go back for follow up tests. The following week when they re-ran the tests they said that the girls had made almost a complete turn around and they sent me home on modified bedrest.

2 months later on Sept 13th I saw Dr. B again (at this point I had been seeing him every week) this time he told me that it appeared that they girls were headed into reverse TTTS and the panic began all over again he said he would call Cincinnati and get back to me. 3 short days later on Sept 16th Diana's water broke, at first I was not sure what had happened other than I stood up and there was a huge gush of blood everywhere, I called my OB and he said to come in right away, when I go there they took me straight back to ultrasound where they determined that Diana was completely folded in half her tiny little chin touching her chest because her water had broken and I had gone into labor.

After what seemed like forever after my doctor had checked me and the ultrasound tech had done the Biophysicals they rushed me across to the hospital (across the catwalk from the Dr.'s office) the immediately rushed me into a c section and put me under general anesthesia, my husband had not yet arrived at the hospital when they had taken me into surgery. It was during the C section that my OB realized that the girls were not headed into reverse TTTS but had completely turned around, baby A was now baby B etc., Elena was delivered first and 1 minute later Diana entered the world both girls were taken to the nursery to be stabilized and to wait for the transport unit from Charleston to arrive.

I remember waking up in recovery and looking out the window and seeing the sky go from grey to black almost instantly, I didn't think much of it since it had rained all day. When they finally took me to my room they told me that the transport team was trying to decide whether to transfer the girls by air or by land due to the weather conditions. I was so groggy I still did not understand what was going on outside, when they wheeled me into postpartum my husband was there and he told me that my mom would stay with me at the hospital and that he would go to CAMC in Charleston to the NICU with the girls.

It was about an hour later the news that it showed a tornado had passed through 7 towns across Ohio and West Virginia, one of those towns being 20 minutes from the hospital and that a man had lost his life trying to save his wife and their dog. It was a lot to take in all at once. 2 days later I was released from the hospital and went to Charleston to be with my girls, from then on it was at the NICU during the week and home and hour and a half away on the weekends.

The girls spent 10 weeks in the NICU before coming home just before their first Thanksgiving. A month later a cold hospitalized Diana for 4 days. But here we are almost 3 years later and other than being developmentally behind I have 2 very healthy identical twin girls, soaring over the obstacles that stand in their way on a daily basis. I have started writing a book about my experience with TTTS and my girls, I have started a March of Dimes team in their honor and have volunteered to help the TTTS Foundation in any way possible. I want to give back to those who helped me and my family get through a very difficult time in our lives, and to emerge stronger than ever and to keep fighting so that one day there will be a cure for TTTS.

Landon and Luke

Amanda Goodman

Landon and Luke's Story

It all started on September 26 2010. Every year my Dad's side of the family has a wonderful family reunion. Lots of homemade food and pies to die for!! My husband and I were chatting with my cousins and they were all asking when we were going to have a baby. Since we had been married a year they all thought it was time. So did God. I ate much more food than normal that day and kept saying oh my gosh everything tastes so good!! A few other things were "off" so on our 2-hour drive home my mind started churning. We got home and I immediately took a pregnancy test. The whole wait 3 mins...HA YEAH RIGHT! I barely set the thing down and it was already showing positive. I hadn't told my husband I was taking one, because I didn't think I was pregnant, so much to my surprise when I was, I said in a partially startled voice "Honey come here." He came in and saw the test sitting there. He said why didn't you tell me?! I explained and we both we baffled by those two pink lines. It didn't sink in for a while. I should add that my husband and I weren't really trying, but we also weren't taking any precautions. My mom had a hard time getting pregnant, so I assumed I would have the same problem.... well you know what happens when you assume

October 4th rolls around and I am at my OB with my husband verifying the pregnancy. The doctor said we were about 6 weeks. She didn't deliver so I went to Northland OBGYN. I had worked with nearly all of these doctors in the practice for about 2 years, so I was comfortable and I knew them on a more personal level. My heart knew it was the right place to go. My appointment for our first ultrasound was October 8th. So, we are in there and the tech does my ultrasound and says "Oh looks like you are having Twins!" I nearly fainted! Twins don't run in my family and my mind couldn't get wrapped around 2 of everything!! She quickly tells me and my husband not to go telling everyone about both, since twins are common early in pregnancy and we could come back in a few weeks and they would be gone. Something was telling me that those two little peanuts weren't going anywhere. We decided to tell my parents and very close friends that we were pregnant, just kept the twin part hush hush. at least till the next ultrasound which was scheduled two weeks later. They were there again (like we knew they would be) but were told again that there was still a chance that one could dissolve. We had another ultrasound at 10 weeks and again our little peanuts were still growing strong! Our doctor told us that they wanted us to be seen by a specialist because we had identical twins and the risks can be a bit higher with them. The sent us to Midwest perinatal to see Dr. Finley. We had an appointment with him around 12 weeks I believe and he checked the growth and such. He told us he wanted to monitor us between 16 and 26 weeks for Twin to Twin Transfusion syndrome. I was so confused and really didn't understand what he was saying. All I heard was 80% chance nothing happens and 20% chance something does. I did understand it was fatal. I am a very positive person so I thought I am not that 20%, everything will be fine.

We were in blissful parent mode and decided all the future things for our babies. We had said that if it was one we wouldn't find out the gender, but if it was Twins we would. Even though I never really wanted to know the gender, I was really excited to pick names. I had picked Lillian Grace after my Great Grandmother and Grandmother, and Lizabeth Jane after my husbands mother. He had picked Landon James after my dad, and Luke William after his dad. We were set! Blissfully unaware of what lied ahead.

Monday December 13th, we went back to see Dr. Finley. I was 16 weeks and 4 days. My mom and Husband went with me. I remember laying there while he scanned my belly, praying that everything would be OK. He mumbled medical terms to the nurse who charted them for him. He had asked how I had been feeling and I said I have so much pressure, I am so uncomfortable. Now this was my first pregnancy, so I had no idea how I should feel, but I knew something was wrong, but didn't know what. Dr. Finley said he was going to check my cervix, but needed to make a important phone call first, without another word he was out the door. My heart was filled with panic. I looked at my mom who looked like she was almost in tears and my husband looked a bit concerned. He came back in and started scanning my belly again. He said see this twin how it can move all over the place...yes. Ok now see this twin how it can hardly move at all and looks basically stuck...yes. This shows me that you have TTTS and I need to get you to a specialist immediately he checked my cervix and told me everything was fine there and I could get dressed. He said he hadn't reached a certain doctor and needed to so he was going to call again while I changed back into my clothes. We went into his office and he said if he couldn't get a hold of this doctor at KU medical center he would be sending us to Utah. I laughed and said Utah?! He said Amanda this is not a laughing matter I am serious. I knew right at once that my babies were in serious danger. KU was never reached while we were at the office, but I gave permission for them to call me and set up an appointment for the next day.

KU called the next day around 9am and asked if we could be there around 11. I said absolutely. My parents and my husband went with me to the consultation where we met Dr. Carl Weiner and his staff at the Center for advanced Fetal care at KU medical center in Kansas City, Kansas. I was getting my sonogram and Dr. Weiner was doing his best to describe to the four of us what we were seeing. We understood that "Baby B" was stuck and that it could die if nothing was done to help it. We were taken into a private room where he told us our options. I have never cried so hard in my life. I was mad and scared all in the same rush of emotion. We were left with two that were comparable but only one was done once and had to be very severe to do twice. Laser

Therapy is what we chose. Our surgery was scheduled for Thursday. We thought for sure they meant the next Thursday and Dr. Weiner said Oh No, if we wait that long you won't have your twins. Thursday couldn't come soon enough! My procedure wasn't until 2 in the afternoon, so not only could I not eat breakfast, but I couldn't have lunch either! UHHHH!!! My hunger pains outweighed my fear, which was a good thing because I was scared to death! So, I had a few sonograms to verify where the babies were. Dr. Weiner was ready and confident of what he needed to do. I was escorted back to the OR by Dr. Weiner and a few nurses. Looking back that was a very special thing he did, it made our connection even stronger. I got into the OR and sat on the table. I couldn't believe how many people were in there for just me and my babies, brings tears to my eyes now just thinking about it. I got tons of blankets because it was freezing, and Dr. Weiner gave the OK for Anesthesia and I was out. Waking up what seemed like days later... I heard Jesse's (my husband) voice and asked if they babies were OK. Dr. Weiner said yes, TWO strong heartbeats!! I got as excited as any drugged-up person could and went back to sleep. I was wheeled back to my room for rest and was told I was going to be picked up in the morning for another scan. Baby A was our recipient and Baby B was our donor. The scans weren't to Dr. Weirner's liking so I was taken back upstairs and was to be brought down in the afternoon to see if anything had changed. Now I should add Dr. Weiner is very particular and if he doesn't like how the baby is acting he will talk to the mother's belly and explain to the baby the situation and tell it to change it plan....it is very comical! My Friday evening scan went ok, still not good enough, so the clinic was opened just for me on Saturday. Dr. Weiner was finally pleased and sent me home Saturday night. Light bed rest and no working until he said so.

Every week for 17 weeks I drove the 20 miles to KU from my home (I am not complaining, this was truly a blessing) never going by myself, cause we never knew what could happen. The babies were growing right on schedule. We had a few hiccups, but nothing to lose sleep over, well at least I didn't because Dr. Weiner assured me that if he was concerned enough I wouldn't be going home. After everything had happened Jesse and I had decided not to find out the genders because we really didn't care what they were, we just wanted both babies. Towards the end, I had a few labor scares which were actually my body just saying to chill out because my uterus couldn't handle all the pressure. I quit working on April 6th, cause my body was just overworked. I was on my feet all day and the doc said no more. I thought oh man I am going to get so much done!! I went to the doctor on Wednesday April 13th. This was weird for us because we usually went on Thursday or Friday. They hadn't "put us on the books" yet, so I wasn't really a patient per the computer. They were just going to have me come in, do my normal scans so that it was in the computer and come back next week at my normal day. I wasn't feeling all that great and couldn't even walk next to my husband anymore because I was waddling so bad I would push him into others in the narrow hall way... I was so big and uncomfortable! I checked in and told the secretary, who had become a good friend, that I was done being pregnant! She said oh Amanda you are doing great you can make it just a bit longer! I sighed and said ok I guess I will! I got my normal sonogram and Dr. Weiner was happen with everything and said to make an appointment for Friday and he left. But something caught out Sonogram Techs eye. Nikole had been our tech from day one, so she knew our babies. She called the Dr. back in and showed him this thing she saw. He ordered a biophysical profile and stress test to be done right then. Baby A passed with flying colors. But Baby B on the other hand didn't pass at all. I was sent to another room to be monitored and there I sat for 45 mins. The nurse came in and out and so did the Dr. He showed me what he was looking at and had decided that we were going to come back on Friday for more scans, but continued the monitoring, just to see. My Dad and husband were there with me and my dad was saying I was going to have the babies by Sunday....Yeah right, I don't think so. Then he said I think you will have them tomorrow... nah I said I don't think so. Not even 2 mins later Dr. Weiner walked in and said your c section is scheduled for 8 am tomorrow morning, you can't go home, you will be wheeled straight upstairs to be monitored for the rest of the evening. My emotions were out of control, well I mean more than a hormonal pregnant woman's would be. The organized person I am I already had my bag packed in the car and only needed my husband to grab a few more things for us. My dad went home and Jesse came upstairs with me. After everything settled down and I was all alone in my room I lost it. It hit me that I would no longer be just Amanda or Jesse's wife. I would be the mother of two little babies that I still had no clue what their genders where. Their little room and little clothes were set up perfectly at home it was just waiting for them. But I knew these babies wouldn't be coming home with me and the unknown really scared me.

    I didn't sleep at all because my mischievous children kept moving off the monitors and so the sweet nurse would come in and readjust and 5 mins later do it again. at one time I had 4 nurses in my room because they couldn't find the baby, it was there just being a little booger. My nurse and I could talk about everything that had happened and she couldn't wait to find out what our little kids were the next day. She let me get off the monitors around 5 am and let me take the longest and hottest shower I wanted. I was so at peace in the shower that morning, never had water felt so good on my swollen belly, I did my best to savor the last few moments for being just Amanda. I got out fixed my hair like I would for any normal day and walked out in my hospital gown ready to meet my babies. My mom laughed at me because I had done my hair and such, but I said well I won't feel like taking a shower tomorrow and pictures will be taken today, so I want to look nice. My OR nurse came around 7 put my catheter in (I wasn't happy about that) and wheeled me to the OR. I am not a fan of needles and was not looking forward to the spinal. I was uncomfortable, in pain, and scared my babies were not going to be alive at birth. Dr. Weiner came over and held my hand and told me everything was going to be fine and I needed to breath and relax so that we could deliver the babies. He assured me that they were fine and if they weren't they would have been delivered hours ago. The Spinal went in and they laid me on the table to fast I thought I was going to fall off. Everything was in a big rush, well at least it felt that way. Jesse came in and everything slowed down. It seemed to take forever to deliver the babies. I told Dr. Weiner that I wanted to know the gender as soon as he saw what they were. I wanted that moment where the doctor said it's a boy or it's a girl! I was so anxious to hear! Shortly after I asked him to tell me he said IT'S A BOY!!! I was so overjoyed! I had that feeling they were boys!! 2 mins later IT'S ANOTHER BOY!!

Landon James was born at 8:18. He weighed 4lbs 6oz and was 16 1/2 inches long. Luke William was born at 8:20. He weighed 3lbs 9oz and was 16 inches long. My boys were alive and well! They spent 48 days (Luke) and 52 days (Landon) in the NICU. Their stay was uneventful! They went home on monitors, which were taken off at their 1 week out of NICU checkup appt! They are now 20 months old and walking talking healthy little boys! They are a joy and are called little miracles by many people.

I know that I had a great team of doctors and nurses during my process and I wish I could give that gift to all TTTS families. I know that have a great doctor doesn't always mean that you will have a perfect outcome, but at least you could look back and say "everyone tried, and gave their all". I feel blessed to be part of a community of such strong people. My children are a blessing, just as any children are, but having my TTTS family has been even more life changing then having my children. I have people around me that "get it" and that makes me feel a little more normal in this crazy world Blessings to all and a wonderful Holiday season to you all!!

Charlie and Kiera

Marcel Pleasance

Marcel represents the United Kingdom. TTTS, like all diseases, knows no geographic boundaries.

His girls had many challenges to overcome along the way. Feeding issues, monitors, Kiera had to have heart surgery for CCHD – all because of TTTS and severe prematurity.

Charlie and Kiera

My wife Emma and I decided we would like another child, after a fifteen year gap between having our other two children, the time was right to start again, my wife became pregnant almost immediately, which was good news I guess but I have to admit i was quite enjoying to trying (wink wink)! My wife took a few home test which were positive, so we booked an appointment at our local doctors. It was confirmed, great news!

Well eight weeks flew by and it was time for our twelve-week routine dating scan. we had joked about it being twins, as I am a twin also, the idea of having twins was exciting but also a bit of a dream really. So in we go for the scan. We had three very big shocks all in one go.

Firstly, we were only eight weeks pregnant not twelve, secondly, we were having twins, and thirdly they were identical. Well I was speechless seriously, we were over the moon about it... A specialist consultant came to see us and explained it wasn't like a normal pregnancy anymore and she would be taking care of my wife and doing the scans etc. from now on ... WOW .... She also told us about complication that there could be with multiple pregnancies, one being TTTS. We were told she would like to see us again in two weeks, so off we went home with greatest news... but with an uneasiness of what might happen.

Two weeks passed and off we went for another scan all excited, not like a usual scan more measuring and taking notes. Two weeks later another scan pretty much the same as the last except this time she told us there were signs of possible TTTS, as the fluid levels were different, and blood flow rate was also different between the placenta and the twins. This got us worrying and a realization of what could be happening hit us hard.

I did a little research on the internet on TTTS and what I found was truly horrific, so I never told my wife all the bad bits , but I saw lots of couples lose one or both twins to this... by sixteen weeks our babies were diagnosed has having TTTS, stage one / two , we were immediately transferred to a specialist fetal medicine unit in the Birmingham Women's hospital UK , under the care of professor Mark Kilby.

At 18 weeks he confirmed TTTS stage two, possibly three, and spoke about our options, one being selective reduction of one twin. This wasn't an option to us, so the next option was laser ablation of the joining vessels between the twins. At 20 weeks we did our usual two hour trip to see the prof, but this time my wife had packed some clothes just in case ..

It was confirmed at that scan something needed to be done, one twin was swimming in an ocean of fluid and our other twin was stuck shrink wrapped to the uterus wall. Laser surgery was scheduled for the next morning.

We had a very sleepless night ... the surgery took about an hour to hour and half, 2 litres of fluid was also removed from around our recipient twin, then came the longest six hour wait ever, until we had a viability scan to see if both girls had made it through ok. Thankfully they had! It was the most amazing news ever and we both cried so much.

After that it was back to weekly scans one week at our local hospital and then the other at Birmingham. All seemed to be going ok until about twenty four weeks, and my wife started showing signs of pre-eclampsia. She was hospitalized at twenty five weeks for bed rest and monitoring, during the many blood tests she had they found that she also has hemophilia c factor eleven deficiency, so it meant her blood doesn't clot well. They transferred us to a regional hospital in Sheffield which has a NICU equipped to accept babies from twenty-four weeks ...

At twenty eight weeks exactly my wife had an emergency c section due to pre-eclampsia, and our girls were delivered ..KIERA was first she was our donor twin weighing 1lb 6oz and then came CHARLIE our recipient twin, two minutes later weighing 1lb 12oz .

My girls spent one hundred and eleven days in NICU, which was an emotional roller coaster for us, but thankfully they're both healthy now and striving every day to hit the big milestones in life!

Adah and Abigail

Heather Pijanowski

If you've been looking for a smooth, happy, fairly uneventful TTTS story, you've finally found one! TTTS is never easy, but I like to share this story in comparison to some of the tough stories to show that you CAN beat the odds and carry until almost full term.

Adah and Abigail

On New Year's Eve 2013, my husband, Brian and I found out we were expecting our 2nd child. We shared the news that night with our family. Our son was only 10 months old at the time so we knew our kids would be close in age, but that's how we wanted it. It wasn't until February 12, 2014 that we found out we were having twins. Brian wasn't there with me when I found out because it was just a dating ultrasound and they had only heard one heartbeat at my 10-week visit. My family tells me I shouldn't be surprised though. There are 15 sets of twins on my father's side of the family, including my grandmother who is an identical twin. I know identical twins aren't supposed to run in families, but in mine there are quite a few.

At the visit the twins were discovered, I was told they were mono/di twins. The ultrasound technician could easily identify the membrane separating the two. I never knew until then that there were different types of twins. I immediately went home and looked up everything I could on mono/di twins. Twin to Twin Transfusion Syndrome (TTTS) was the first and biggest thing that came up. I read up on it, got to know it, knew my doctors were checking for it, and put it in the back of my mind because things like this don't happen to people like me.

Things like TTTS don't happen to people like me, until they do.

On Friday, April 4, 2014, Brian and I went in for our anatomy scan. We were 18 weeks exactly. After the scan was done, the technician went to get the doctor. We knew at that point that something wasn't right. The doctor came in and proceeded to tell us that we were at a stage 0. At a stage 0 we didn't technically qualify at TTTS but the fluid levels of the girls were different enough that we needed to be monitored more closely. We would need to come back in in one week to see where we were. We talked to the Care Coordinator with St. Luke's to discuss the possibility of laser ablation surgery in Seattle, Washington. She was going to go ahead and send all of our information over to them just in case.

Later that evening, I got a phone call from Melissa from Evergreen Medical Center in Washington. She made a horrifying ordeal seem manageable. While talking to her, a sense of calm swept over me. I knew I could handle this. By the end of the conversation, she was telling us that we should go ahead and pack bags and get things in order for plane tickets and a hotel room, just in case.

We did not have another visit until the following Wednesday. That was a very long five days filled with tears, suitcases and possible travel plans.

Our "just in case" came on Wednesday, April 9th, 2014. During our scan, it was very clear something was wrong. Both girls' fluids were just within "acceptable" range, but Baby B (our donor) did not have a visible bladder. During that visit, we were told we were going to Seattle. We needed to leave later that day to have surgery on Friday. Because of all the preparation Melissa had helped us with, we had a game plan. We called all of our parents. My Father-in-law booked our flight and set up our hotel, my Mother-in-law set up a spot for our dogs at the kennel and my parents made sure they were home to take our son for the weekend.

We got to Seattle around 11pm Wednesday night. Just enough time to find something to eat and try to sleep. The next morning, we met the team we would be working with and had an ultrasound to see how things had progressed. In the matter of a day, our donor had lost almost all fluid; she was officially "stuck."

We spent the rest of the day touring Seattle and trying to keep our minds off the next day. Friday morning, I was 19 weeks along. We went to the hospital and I was prepped for surgery. Donna and the rest of the team, once again, made us feel like this was routine and we had nothing to worry about. Watching the doctor perform the surgery was truly amazing, even more amazing was being able to wee the little hands and feet of our little (stubborn) girl, who kept trying to play with the instrument the doctor was using to separate the blood vessels of the placenta. We had 17 connections, the most our surgeon Dr. Walker had seen was 23.

That evening was possibly the scariest of the whole ordeal. We knew we had done everything in our power to save our girls, but now we just had to wait to see if they survived the surgery. That evening in the hospital was filled with gratefulness, tears, fear, anxiety, and very little sleep.

I remember that morning being difficult as well. They did not do the ultrasound until 10am. Brian and I were both so jittery waiting for Dr. Walker to start the ultrasound. All we wanted to hear was two heartbeats. Thankfully, Dr. Walker seemed to know that. He put the wand on my stomach and within seconds he announced, "There's one heartbeat and there're two heartbeats." We felt relieved and shed a few tears. We were cautiously optimistic as we were told the next two weeks were the most critical.

We made it through those two weeks and all the way to 35 weeks, and on August 1, 2014, Baby A, Miss Adah, decided it was time to meet her parents. Baby B, Miss Abigail, followed five minutes after her big sister. We spent 9 and 10 days respectively in the NICU and then came home to begin their job of terrorizing their big brother, Luke.

Today, they are happy, healthy little girls. All thanks to St. Luke's Hospital in Kansas City, Missouri for their close monitoring and Dr. Walker and his staff at Evergreen Maternal Fetal Medicine in Washington for their amazing care, and our family and friends for being willing to jump into action on short notice when we needed them most.

Many cases of TTTS don't have the smooth outcome that ours did, but it is possible.

Grady and Hudson

Lori Cobb

My husband, Nick and I, were married about 5 years before we started trying to have a family. I always thought that it would be easy to get pregnant but that was certainly not the case for us. After months of infertility, we went through testing and ultimately found out that the only way was going to be able to get pregnant was through IVF. Before we could do IVF, my husband had to endure months of injections multiple times a week and a procedure to extract his sperm.

We started our IVF journey in Oct 2011, our cycle went per the doctor's text book perfect. Due to our cycle being so successful, our doctors encourage us to just transfer 1 embryo due to high likelihood of a multiple pregnancy. We agreed since we didn't think we were prepared to have twins. Apparently, God has an awesome sense of humor and at our first ultrasound at 7 weeks; we were shocked to find out that we were expecting identical twins. Our fertility doctors set us up for an OB/Gyn appointment and explained identical twins were high risk and we needed to be monitored to see is they were Mono/Mono or Mono/di. He even discussed TTTS but stated that it was a rare condition.

At 11 weeks pregnant, we had our first OB/Gyn appointment and he was unable to see a membrane separating the boys and deemed me too high risk and referred me to a MFM. At 14 weeks, we had our first MFM appointment with Dr. Wendel. Thankfully, during that appointment they could see a membrane separating the boys. Dr. Wendel explained even though he found a membrane, I was to be monitored at minimum of every 2 weeks.

At our 16-week appointment, we found out we were having boys! Dr. Wendel expressed his concern about the boys' fluid levels. Grady, baby A, had more fluid than Hudson, baby B. Dr. Wendel stated there was just a slight difference and wanted me to come back in a week. Due to a holiday, it was almost 2 weeks before my next appointment putting me barely at 18 weeks. I went into that appointment a little nervous, as the ultrasound tech started measuring fluids. She was normally very talkative but that day it was different. I asked her several times if everything was ok and all she would tell me is Dr. Wendel would be in a moment to explain.

Dr. Wendel came in and sat down and held my hand and asked me the scariest question, how far would I go to save my babies lives? I told him with no hesitation, I would do anything. He told me the boys were suffering from twin to twin transfusion syndrome and we needed to act fast if we were going to save their lives. He showed me how much fluid Grady, baby A, had and Hudson, baby B, had little to no fluid around him. He looked like he was stuck and the membrane that separated them was saran-wrapped around him.

Dr. Wendel asked me how quickly Nick and I could get to Houston. I remember looking at him dumbfounded. I knew that TTTS was a risk but I never imagine that we would have to travel out of state for treatment. Dr. Wendel explained there were only about 12 different places in the country that could treat our condition and Houston was our best option. I told Dr. Wendel we would fly out immediately but I needed to call my husband. I called Nick and we decided and in less than 10 hours we were in Houston checking into the hospital.

It was after 7pm by time I got checked in and as the nurse walked me into the room. Dr. Johnson was sitting there waiting on me. He immediately started my ultrasound. He stated that I did have TTTS and was stage 3C. He stated that we would need surgery the next day and went over everything including mortality rates. 0% chance of survival with no surgery. 80% chance one baby would make it and 40% chance that both boys would survive. I remember the nurse giving Ambien to help me sleep that night but even with that both I and Nick got very little sleep.

The next day, I had surgery and they severed all the blood vessels the boys shared and took 1 ½ liters of fluid out of Grady sac to give Hudson a chance to recover. Dr. Johnson stated that he had to give the boys unequal placental share, Grady had 75% and Hudson had 25% and that the next 24 hours were critical and he would do an ultrasound first thing the next morning. The following morning, we had our ultrasound and we still had 2 heartbeats. Dr. Johnson stated that we passed the most critical stage but we would need to be seen weekly by Dr. Wendel to monitor growth, especially for Hudson our donor. He also stated at some point Hudson would stop growing due to his lack of placental share. I followed back up with Dr. Wendel for the next 2 weeks and I was finally released to go back to work.

For the next 10 weeks, I saw Dr. Wendel weekly for ultrasounds and was elated every time to see 2 heart beats. At week 30, I had fetal echo on the boys' heart and growth scans, Dr. Wendel came in told me he had good news and bad news. The good news was both boys' heart looked great but the bad news was Hudson had not grown any in the last 2 weeks. Per my growth scan there was almost 50% discordance between Grady and Hudson. Dr. Wendel stated he no longer felt comfortable with me being outpatient and that he wanted me to be on hospital bed rest for the remainder of my pregnancy. I made it exactly 1 week on hospital bed rest and at 31 weeks, I failed my NST and Dr. Wendel came up to my room and told me that Hudson was showing signs of distress and we needed to deliver that day. On Wednesday, May 23, 2012 at 8:27 pm, we welcomed Grady Lee and Hudson David into the world. Grady was 3lb9oz and Hudson was 1lb13 oz. We had a rather uneventful NICU stay. Grady came home after 41 days and Hudson 51 days.

Our Life after TTTS

Though our NICU stay was uneventful, the weeks and months that followed were anything but. I thought as soon as we were home from the NICU that TTTS would be a thing of the past. I didn't realize how TTTS has forever changed our lives. Grady fortunately thrived and gained weight with no problem. Grady had developmental delay but most of that was from prematurity. Hudson on the other hand almost immediately started having problems. He was diagnosed with severe reflux and was placed on medicine. None of the medicine that prescribed seems to work so we were referred to a pediatric GI specialist. After 2 back to back hospitalizations for failure to thrive, Hudson had an ng tube placed in his nose to help supplement his feeding.

That winter Hudson faced 3 more hospitalization with the last one being with aspiration pneumonia. The medical team thought it would be in Hudson best interest to be strictly ng tub fed for a month to allow his body to recover from the pneumonia. When we finally were given the ok to start oral feeds again, Hudson had lost the ability to take a bottle and a more permanent G-tube was placed and all kinds of testing began to see why he wouldn't eat and why he chronically threw up.

During this time, I worked diligently to get both Grady and Hudson tested for services. After months of paperwork and requests, I finally could get both Grady and Hudson in development center to receive services. They are now active, healthy 2 ½ year olds and still receive PT, OT, and Speech but are both making great strides in all 3 areas. Grady is on track to test out in the next year and Hudson may not be far behind him. Hudson also sees an oral feeding specialist and we are slowly seeing improvement. Eventually, Hudson went from chronically throwing up 4-6 times a day to rarely throwing up thanks to a blended diet using real food instead of a pre-made formula. After that, Hudson went from refusing to eat to eating soft foods such as applesauce and yogurt.

I thought as soon as we had our boys our TTTS journey would be over, little did I know how much it would affect us even 3 years later. TTTS is a horrible disease and there are too many lives that are forever changed by it. My hope and prayer is that we finally find a cure for this disease. As much as I hate TTTS, I am thankful for the many friends that I have met due to our TTTS journey. I am also grateful that my faith in God and marriage is stronger than ever. Lastly but not least, I am blessed beyond measure to have 2 little boys that survived TTTS.

William and Mason

Susan Napolitano Turner

My name is Susan Napolitano Turner. I'm a 37-year-old mother of 2 sets of identical twins. My first set (William and Mason) had TTTS, and are both survivors. This is their story, well our story.

Matt and I had a beautiful wedding on December 13, 2008 and we honeymooned in Philly for Monday night football. I had almost the entire month of December off, and by the time I went back to work in January I already knew I was pregnant. I had my first doctor's appointment the first week in February. I was 8 weeks pregnant. I was getting weighted and blood pressure taken when the nurse look at me and said "You are lucky, you are seeing Dr. P, and she does ultrasounds at the first appointments. I was so excited I was going to see my baby!!!!! The appointment was going along as routine (I guess it's my first baby) and she is getting ready to do the ultrasound. I have a tilted uterus so she had to do the internal ultrasound (If you don't know what that is, let's just say you can't move at all) She says there is your baby's heartbeat! It was a blob with a flicker I really couldn't move to look at the screen. She was still doing the ultrasound (I didn't think anything about it, again first baby) when my sister who was in the room says "there's another baby isn't there?" Dr. P said yes but I having trouble finding it's heartbeat, oh the panic that went through my body. "There it is! She says. You are having Twins! I was in complete shock!

At 16 weeks I gained 12 pounds in one month. Dr. C asked if my appetite changed in anyway. I said no not really but I do eat pop tarts every morning. Dr. C said to only eat one instead of both of them and then set me up for my 20-week ultrasound where we would find out the sex of the babies. I was sent to Dr. C's husband who is a prenatal specialist. At my appointment, I was told they were boys and that they looked good. We were told about TTTS at that time, they explain to us what would happen if the boys would have TTTS. We were told the Cincinnati's Children's Hospital had a Fetal Care Center so we would not have to travel for any of our appointments. They wanted to see me in one month and at that time we would also meet with a pediatrician cardiologist.

At 24 weeks, I was told the boys had TTTS, William (Donor) was stuck and had only 2cm of fluid around him. Mason (Recipient) had 8 cm of fluid around him and his heart was showing signs of strain. I had a MRI and Echo done and then met with a group of doctors. We were told we were stage III and that we were a candidate for either the fetalscopic laser photocoagulation (SFLP) procedure or amino reduction. We had 3 days to decide since I was 25 + weeks and surgery can't be done after 27 weeks. We decided on laser that day and it was scheduled for the following week. I had my steroid shots and all my testing and was ready to go for surgery on June 11th.

The surgery was early in the morning; I was awake for the whole thing. It was the worst experience I ever been though in my 30 years. It didn't last as long as I thought it would. When the doctor finished, he informed me that the laser surgery was not able to be performed because my amniotic fluid started to leak into my abdominal cavity and my uterus shrunk so they had to stop the procedure. I was transported via ambulance from Children's to Good Samaritan Hospital. I was passed 24 weeks and the babies were viable so if I went into labor they would have delivered the babies. I was in so much pain from the procedure (ammonic fluid leaking) I couldn't really move. They had some trouble finding both heartbeats at Good Sam when I first arrived. I thought nothing of it I just thought the babies weren't cooperating. I wasn't told that the hours immediately following the surgery were crucial and that there was a chance of losing one or both of my babies. I thought since the surgery was done we were in the clear. They eventually found both heart beats, everyone was very relieved. The next morning an ultrasound was done and both boys had urine in their bladders, their fluid was more equal and Mason's (recipient) heart was looking good. I didn't need to have the laser surgery and since I was too far along my only option was to have more amniotic reeducations if necessary. I was sent home on bed rest and I was to have ultrasounds twice a week and monthly echoes. They were hoping I could carry the boys to 32 weeks

On August 8, 2009 (34 weeks) at 7:42 pm William Matthew was born weighing 5lbs., 10 oz. and at 7:43 pm Mason Wright was born weighing 6 lbs., 8 oz. Both boys were healthy only needing to be in the NICU over night because I had hemorrhage. We went home after 3 days in hospital. William and Mason are healthy children. I am very grateful for all the doctor and nurses at Cincinnati Children's' and Good Samaritan Hospital for making that happen.

Cody and Christian

Andrew Chase

We were diagnosed with Twin-to-Twin Transfusion Syndrome at 21 weeks. We first tried an amnioreduction and when that didn't work we elected for the laser surgery. There was one local hospital, Abbott Northwestern, that has done these surgeries. They had done about 26 surgeries and told us there was about 80% chance that one baby would survive and 33% both would survive. We were also told about Children's Hospital in Cincinnati by this hospital and the clinic that diagnosed us. The doctor at Abbott told us to not pick one for convenience (this way if something happened we wouldn't be wondering if we did everything possible).

We spoke with Cincinnati by telephone and immediately felt comfortable with them. They had done over 600 cases and had a 93-93% survival rate of one baby, 68-70% for both! We were assigned to a case worker, Lisa, who was able to answer all of our questions and give us an idea of what to expect when we arrived in Cincinnati. We drove down, had a day of testing and the surgery the following day. The hardest part for me during the surgery was being alone in waiting room 18 hours away from my family and friends. The surgery took about 30-45 min longer than expected due to the fact that some blood had gotten into the amniotic fluid and made it cloudy where they couldn't see so they had to do a fluid exchange. After the surgery I got to meet with the doctors so they could tell me how it went. Before I spoke to them, they wheeled Amanda to the room so I could see her. She was bawling when I saw her, my heart sank. I was sure we had lost one or both of the babies, but was relieved when I saw the doctors smiling and saying it was just the drugs wearing off and that she missed me, both babies had 10 toes and 10 fingers and were doing great. They took care of 35 blood vessel connections that were connected and one additional that was close enough that they thought it may connect at some point.

The twins were born early and spent about a month in the NICU. Cody was our Recipient and he has had a heart murmur from birth, but it is almost completely repaired itself. Christian was our Donor and he has had more health issues. He had a hernia repair done when he was about a month old and also spent 3 days in the hospital when he was diagnosed with Reactive Airway Disorder. Christian is on average about 3 pounds lighter and about an inch shorter than Cody. We'll see if that persists throughout childhood. Development wise, they are on track and are two very happy boys.

We have two older boys, Jasper and Vincent. The hardest part for them throughout the entire pregnancy and NICU stay was the 8 days we were in Ohio. They were safe at Grandma and Grandpa's house, but missed us badly after a few days. We'd call them every day and they always asked when we were going to be home. They still get worried when they sleep over at someone's house that we are going to be gone for an extended period again. They are great big brothers, Vincent (our second oldest) knew from day one that we were going to have twin boys. He pointed at Christian in the womb well before we knew about anything and said that was going to be his little brother and the other was going to be Jasper's little brother. And the crazy thing about it is that Christian and Vinny are so much alike and Cody and Jasper are so much alike!

I would have to say the worst thing we heard during our diagnosis/pregnancy was form one of the first doctors that we spoke to recommended that we do a selective termination and abort one of the babies so one could survive. We knew in our hearts that there must be another choice and I'm glad we were given the 4 options of, Amnioreduction, Laser Surgery, Termination or do nothing. We prayed to God we would be able to meet these 2 miracle babies and they complete our family.

We were also told not to "google" TTTS or we would see just horror stories, but in reality, I think they should have told us about the TTTS foundation website. Mary Slaman does an amazing job of outreach and getting moms in contact with the right people. We found out about the foundation towards the end of the pregnancy and have continued to stay in touch with them. We now try and reach out to as many people as we can that are newly diagnosed, especially if they live close to us. I had to take over the role of both mom and dad while my wife was on strict bed rest and it was hard. Luckily I had family and friends that helped out and bring me meals and help with our boys, so we try and do this for other moms and dads.

We also were glad to go to Twins Days in Twinsburg Ohio in 2014 for the 25th anniversary of the foundation with many other families. It was nice to put faces to the names that have helped give their support.

We felt like we were meeting old friends. I wish I would've known some of these people during our 8 days in Ohio as some of them lived close and we could've used the support. We still need their support today and we are a close family.

Jordan and Eli

Penny and Anthony were thrilled to learn they were expecting twins, which would round their family out to six children.

However, at the 22 week appointment, their doctor informed them that one of the babies was bigger than the other. Penny and her husband didn't know what that meant, but later received the TTTS diagnosis from a different doctor in Minneapolis.

Penny began researching like crazy to find out all she could about TTTS. What she found really scared her:

- TTTS has a high mortality rate.
- Sometimes the donor twin (Elijah) dies from the loss of blood or from having too small of a share of the placenta to receive necessary nutrients –
- Sometimes the recipient twin (Jordan) dies from heart failure.
- Without treatment, most babies with TTTS will

die, and many TTTS babies have long term health issues

Jordan was getting too much blood and his heart was enlarged. Elijah was pushed up against the side of the uterus because of all of the excess fluid in the other twin's sac. Elijah was "shrink wrapped" in his sac, meaning there was literally no extra room in the sac.

Penny and Anthony made weekly trips to Minneapolis for ultrasounds. Eventually, the travel became so much of a burden that Penny made the trips alone so that Anthony could stay home and care for the children.

The family had few treatment options.

Placental laser surgery to destroy the connecting vessels was one choice. However, because Elijah "had a bad cord insertion" they feared he would not tolerate the surgery, and risked passing away. Another option presented to them was a selective cord coagulation - by coagulating one of the umbilical cords to stop the blood flow, resulting in the death of one twin to save the other. This was not an option to Penny and Anthony.

The third option, and what Penny chose to pursue, was amnio reduction. During this process, excess amniotic fluid from the sac of the recipient twin is removed using a needle to help balance fluid levels.

These procedures can be very painful, and usually result in a large amount of fluid withdrawn. Penny had to have this done two times in her pregnancy.

In between the two amnioreductions, Penny recalls being very large from the excess fluid building up.

Penny spent time on bed rest, spending hours on her side, which is supposed to help the donor twin receive nutrients, and she drank lots of protein shakes. Protein has been shown to improve the outcome for the babies.

Death was a constant concern. Penny was afraid to buy anything to prepare for the babies, just in case they didn't make it.

At 31 weeks and 5 days Elijah's heart rate rapidly decelerated, and an emergency C-section was performed. No one believed he would make it, but both babies were born alive, weighing 2 pounds, 12 ounces and 4 pounds, 14 ounces. They were breathing on their own and didn't even need ventilators.

Jordan spent 16 days and Eli 27 days in the Special Care nursery.

Evelyn and Elizabeth

Lyndsay Brown

I took a pregnancy test two days before my birthday, wanting to know if i could have that margarita. I immediately came out and told my husband Jesse, "No margarita for me!"

I made an appt with my OB because I started to spot a little and was concerned. We had an ultrasound at 6 weeks. The doctor asked me if I was taking fertility drugs or something, which I thought was a strange question. When I replied no and, he told me that I had three sacs, but only two have heartbeats.

We were shocked! We were expecting triplets? My OB explained that I was spotting because I miscarried one of them and he was concerned about the other babies. We had to come back in four days. Jesse kept flipping through a magazine he was "reading" and looking at me in a WEIRD WAY. Twins ?? Great!!!! yay!!!

Thankfully when we returned four days later the

other babies were both doing awesome. Two strong heartbeats--we were having twins!

But there was still concern that there was no membrane separting the two and the possiblity of TTTS.

I had an appointment two weeks later, and found out they could be MO-MO twins, meaning that they share everything and are in the same sac. This is a pretty dangerous situation. But thankfully, a week later or so when we returned they were able to see a membrane separating them.

At our next check up we found out the sex. GIRLS! But then we got the bad news. They did indeed have the Twin to Twin Transfer Syndrome.

A few days later I went to urgent care because my face was swelled up like I had an allergic reaction to something. In actuality my blood pressure was super high and I had +3 protien in my urine, signs of preeclampsia, but my doctor said it was too early for that. I was only twenty weeks pregnant. My BP was checked again a few days later, and since it was higher than before, I was taken to the hospital and told the terrible news that I might have to deliver if the situation declined further.

Naturally, I was very upset. My OB told me that we can have more babies but not if I died. I was so upset. We had to cancel plans with Jesse's family and they came to the hosptial instead.

Thankfully, my health improved over night and I was referred to a matrnal fetal specialist. The MFM explained to me that I had several options at this point. Termination, wait it out (there was a high chance that I could lose both babies with this option), or fly to Seattle, Wa for an ablation surgery. We went for the surgery. We had to try something!

My sugery was at Evergreen Hospital with Dr. Walker. Before we headed into surgery, we decided to name the girls. Just in case anything happened, I wanted them to have names. We named Baby A Faith and Baby B Hope. We stopped in the Chapel before and prayed. I was getting ready to go into surgery and Jesse asked if Dr. Walker would pray with us and he did.

I had the surgery at 7pm at night (it was supposed to be at 1pm) and I have never felt so sick. It had been 24hrs since I had eaten anything. After surgery, I had vitals my checked, but they did not check the babies at that point. After 24 hours, they finally checked on the babies and we were surprised to learn the TTTS had reversed and the twins were doing better. They both had good strong heartbeats! Before, twin B--the donor twin (Elizabeth) didn't have a bladder or kidneys, and she was showing great improvement.

I was in Seattle for about 5 days. I was put on some

meds to stop contractions if I had them.

After the surgery, I had a hard time eating and gaining wieght. I had to be on strict bedrest and in and out of the hospitals all the time from 19 weeks until delivery at 36 weeks. Everything I did was for the babies then.

I made it to 36 weeks, amazingly. The girls were delivered November 3rd 2009 at 9am, at Memorial Central Hospital, Colorado Springs, CO.

Hearing their cries were the best thing ever that I have heard!! I cried, and everyone told me to calm down. Evelyn Faith was born 5lb 7oz, Elizabeth Hope was 5lb even. Elizabeth had some trouble breathing, but they both were only in NICU for 5 hours, and then they got to come home with me after 4 days in the hospital :)

They are now healthy little girls and doing well. I am thankful they are here with us and I am SO glad I did not choose to terminate. I am a strong beliver in the power of prayer! I have Jesse's Aunt Liz (Elizabeth is named after her) to thank mostly, because she was there in the ups and downs of the pregnancy, and now, she is looking down on us from heaven.

I cannot thank everyone enough with all the help we received through this ordeal. Jesse's mom came and helped when Jesse had to go to his tour duty with the Air Force. We were lucky that he was wanted at the Air

Force Academy in Colorado Spring so he was able to come home at night and take me to hospital when needed. When his mom had to go home, his Aunt Liz from Virgina came and stayed with us for a long time, about two and a half months. She died from a battle with cancer, in Januar 2015. She will always be in our hearts.

It was such a blessing to have help with our other daughter Emma. We also had a lot of help from friends and members from our church come help us with meals and house cleaning when mom and aunt Liz had to leave. Thankfully, we were never without help.

Part Three
Double Loss

Double Loss

Hands down, this is the most difficult section of the book to read, but I believe it is one of the most important. We have mentioned several times throughout the book how many babies die each year from TTTS. The number is believed to be exponentially higher since babies miscarried before 20 weeks don't "count". We need to make them count.

We must make them count.

Some of the double loss mamas have been the most active in bringing about awareness, change, and support for the TTTS community. I encourage you to read each of their stories, and to remember their babies always.

        Jackalyn and Alexa
        Catherine and Hattie
        Matias and Mael
        Alana and Selena
        Heatherly Rose and Winter
        Allanah and Liz

Jackalyn and Alexa

Andrea Clark Ross

My friend Andrea's twins were born too early, and neither survived. Since then, Andrea has been a major part of the TTTS Support Community, and each year organizes the effort to send out Mother's Day Cards to moms from their TTTS angels, and going through the process of growing and building the TTTS Suport Team into a 501(c)3 organization.

Sharing the stories of other mothers who have gone through the nightmare of TTTS can be so incredibly heartbreaking. But we do it for awareness. And the hope that the awareness we are sharing may help save even ONE family from the heartbreak we have experienced is good enough!

Those who write the stories do it to heal. To honor their children, here or in heaven, and to share with everyone those precious babies who are so important to us.

I have become friends with so many amazing women who, despite the most horrendous loss of losing one or both babies, have gone on to do incredible things. Andrea, despite suffering such a horrendous loss, organized a huge drive for donations of bears, buttons, ribbons, and money for the Molly Bear organization. This wonderful charity sends bears to grieving mothers, specially designed to weigh the same amount as the baby lost. I am waiting for my Kathryn bear to arrive, and I can't wait!

Andrea has decided that she is ready to share the story of her beautiful girls, Jackalyn and Alexa.

Jackalyn and Alexa - Too Soon to the Party by Andrea

May 2012 was a stressful month, lots of travel from our home in North Carolina to family in Tennessee, to see my stepson in NJ and back all in about 20 days. It hadn't been a great trip and I had smashed my face on the side of a roller coaster cracking a tooth. So, I felt horrible, truly miserable, not really noticing when that time of the month came and went.... with no sign of evil red. After a particularly bad reaction to a work-related encounter with a dead body I clued in.

I swear that first pregnancy test took forever to

confirm, I woke my poor husband up after only an hour of sleep because I was crying so hard. I had always wanted to be a mommy. While the shock was still fresh I went to the dentist for that pesky tooth. Infected, so on to penicillin I went, and on came the puking. Nothing would stay down and after 3 straight days the dentist advised me to go to the ER afraid that the infant might have been harmed by the penicillin.

Panicked my husband and I went, we had only told a couple of friends and my mother we were expecting. My family has a strong history of miscarriage and I was determined to not get excited till 12 weeks. In the ER they wouldn't let my husband into the ultrasound. and I laid on that cold table in tears, "Please" I kept whispering to the tech "Please just tell me there's still a heartbeat" I was 7 weeks so I knew it might be hard to get. "shh" said the tech "I'm concentrating". So, I cried, I was convinced that sure enough I had lost this child already.

Finally the tech said "I'm not supposed to show you this, but here." She turned the monitor my way and said "Here is Baby A, and here is Baby B". I think at that point I cried harder! No history in the family, no fertility drugs, no clue what the next 5 months would hold.

That was by far not my only trip to the ER with my bundles of "joy" :) I was sick every 45 mins for 8 weeks running. 30 pounds and several hospital stays later at 15 weeks finally I got to start enjoying my pregnancy. 18 weeks came and we had running bets among the family about boys, girls or both! On our way into "sexting" Ultrasound we joked about names and how much longer I would be able to waddle around. I was already measuring almost 30 weeks around!

GIRLS!! Twin A would be Alexa, Twin B Jackalyn... and oh "by the way we think you might have a touch of TTTS but nothing to worry about... we will just send you for a better ultra sound at the university 90 mins away." - Um, what?? HHrrmmm google: "what is TTTS?" My husband had to go to work so I had googled out of sheer curiosity, after all he had said it was nothing to worry about. I had a full-on panic attack when I read the first page to pop up. WiKi "TTTS is 90% fatal to one or both infants" I called my sister in law in such a panic her husband called mine because neither one could understand me. My husband official band me from googling while he was at work. :-)

My midwife the next day knew nothing about Twin To Twin Transfusion Syndrome, even though she carried twins herself, and in fact offered us a consult to terminate. I've never been so hysterical in my life. Didn't these people understand! I just needed a real doctor! My babies needed a real doctor! Luckily the nurse at the practice took pity on me and made my appointment at the University for the next day, transfer effective immediately.

18 weeks, Pre-stage 1 TTTS confirmed. Jackalyn was our donor, in 2 cm of fluid "stuck" to the uterine wall just under my ribs, Alexa our recipient, 9 cm of fluid cradled in our ribs. Watch, wait, see... weekly Ultrasounds, but the rotating Neonate specialist said "This is probably going to get worse before it gets better, you need to start preparing to be sent to CHOP for surgery".

See my husband is a paramedic and I volunteer with EMS as well. We had a working knowledge of TTTS, could understand what all the treatments might entail medically. Most importantly we knew the odds were against us, this was going to be a fight my body and the bodies of my girls would have to fight, we were simply passengers on this ride.

Week 19 was good, seemed the fluids had evened out to 3cm and 5cm for the girls. We started to get hopeful, I slogged through making a registry, enjoyed just floating in the pool and helped by sweet husband plan a nursery. But I was tired, and boy was I getting big fast! Week 20, Friday I measured almost 34 weeks, was in a pregnancy brace and in pain. Not sore but in pain. So much so I couldn't sit still for the ultra sound well. As soon as they touched the wand to my hard belly I knew. The fluids had changed again, drastically, Jackalyn was still in 2 cms of fluid but Alexa was now in 13cm and was now head down on my cervix.

I remember saying "No no little girl, your too early for the party! Stay in there a bit please!"

No wonder I hurt so much. We had yet another rotating Neonate who said that fluids were high but that everything else with the girls looked fine so they didn't want to screw with anything just yet. No amnio reduction just yet, lets see how the weekend went and come back on Wednesday to check... Disappointed and with a horrible feeling I just couldn't explain we drove the 90 mins home and I tried to relax.

By Sunday night I knew something was wrong, I was spotting fluid and the discomfort in my hips was getting intense. So back up to the hospital we went. Now technically 21 weeks we went to Labor and Delivery complete with hospital bag, expecting to have a long stay. Nope, after several hours and two pelvic exams the hospital said my body was just responding to the fluids building, both test had come back negative that the fluid was amniotic and I would go home. No Ultra Sound would be needed and so Flexerile was prescribed to ease the cramping in my back....

But nothing helped. Monday and Tuesday are a blur

nothing but pain sticks out. I couldn't sit, stand, or lay down for more then 30 – 45 minutes without the pain intensifying. I remember the times distinctly. See I never got sick or upset while my husband was home, it always happened while he was at work. 24 very long hours pacing a two-bedroom apartment that seemed to shrink with every min.

8:10pm - Tornado warnings throughout the county, husband dispatched to another car accident, I think 'maybe a bath will help'.

8:15 – 8:27: Bath water stops all the pain, blissful silence rains through my body and I hold my breath hopping this has finally passed.

8:30 – My world falls apart as I stand up out of the bath and blood runs over the white bath rug. Finally, I realize I've been in labor for hours, 100% back labor, no contractions, no ups and downs like I've always been told labor happens. Just white hot pain up my spine and blood all over the bathroom.

911 was not an option, my husband was 911 and he was helping sick hurt people. Luckily, I had a friend, the wife of my husband's partner who had asked earlier if I wanted company. A fellow paramedic. I called her and through the wind and rain she came, I didn't tell her I was bleeding till after she helped me into the car.

She too knew. Our closest hospital has no NICU, and

at 21 weeks I knew they wouldn't life flight my girls to the University 40 minutes away.... Through my blinding pain and fear I had to figure out how to say good bye, how to get a hold of my husband.

9:45 - we arrived at the hospital, and as they helped me into a wheelchair I saw my husband's ambulance arrive as well. He had a critical patient too, he would come when he was able.

10:30 –Husband is able to come up for a moment, assures me that he will be back as soon as he finds someone to cover the county, you see he was the ONLY paramedic on duty that night. He kissed me and passed the doctor on his way in to examine me in the hall.

3 minutes later the Worst doctor in the world pronounces "Your 5cms dilated and fully effaced, there is nothing we can do. You need to prepare to welcome your girls."

Welcome? How could I welcome babies I would never know? How could they not try to stop this labor?? Something!!! In my anxiety and with my blood pressure rising I black out.

Later I would find out that they ultra-sounded me in my blacked-out state, found I was now at 27.5cms of fluid but that both girls, both beautiful perfect girls were kicking and happy and so very alive.

I remember waking up to my husband holding my

hand, silent tears rolling down his cheeks as he held me saying "It's going to be OK baby, I love you, they can't stop it. Andrea, the girls have to come now." I calmed somehow, knowing he was there, having his arms around me. He would get to see the birth of his little girls.

1:44 am September 19th 2012 21 weeks 2 days - My body must have heard the message too because with one finally white hot searing jolt up my spine Alexa made her entrance into the world by soaking the entire nursing staff assisting me. One minute later Jackalyn made a slightly smaller splash into the world. And all was calm.

The best thing I ever did was hold my girls that night, cuddle them, cry over them, take pictures of them, spend this heart tearing, soul breaking all consuming pain with my husband. He will never know them as I did, will never love them as I do. But still we hold each other together. Because in such a pit of despair and pain if we don't hold each other together we will both fall apart. Our girls may not be here screaming for bottles or cooing and giggling music to our ears but they have brought my husband and I together in ways nothing sort of surviving such a horror could.

Somehow, I knew we would never bring our girls home. My husband had worried about only having a two seat-er truck, about fitting two cribs in our apartment. Two weddings, two proms, 3 women in a the house all on the same cycle :-) And my only reply was ever "Lets worry when they get here". Like somehow I knew that to worry while they were with us spinning and tumbling in my tummy would be a waste of time.

We chose not to bury our girls and instead held a small memorial on the beach for them since really, they were ours alone. We continue to talk about them and do things in memory of them daily. I carry them with me everywhere, in a necklace with their ashes, and in a tattoo the exact print of their tiny feet. Never will I be without them.

Now my girls walk beside me as I try and help other moms. Every day I try to help other moms dealing with TTTS or comfort moms who now hold angels in their hearts. Not what I thought I would spend my days doing 5 months past their due date. But for now I find peace in what I hope makes Alexa and Jackalyn Proud.

My husband in turn has hooked up with an organization that does bereavement photos for stillborn and NEONATAL deaths called Now I Lay Me Down to Sleep, trying to give other families one of the things we hold most dear, photos of their angels. He has started a company called "2 of a Kind Photography" and uses the purple daisies I have adopted as their symbol for his logo.

Never will I allow the world to forget that my girls lived, never will I allow myself to believe that this pain is all I have left to remember them by.

Catherine and Hattie

Emily Farwell

Emily really made an impression on me because rather than letting her grief from losing her identical twin daughters completely consume her, she began a photo project in their honor. I know so many people have found joy in finding a beautiful place, taking a picture of it, and putting Catherine and Hattie's names on the picture.

I admire Emily's strength and faith. I admire her desire to comfort others when it is she who deserves to be comforted. And of course, we both lost a Kathryn/Catherine.

Catherine and Hattie

Twin to Twin Transfusion Syndrome. I had never heard of it before I was faced with it. Now I am spreading awareness about it and the tragic effects it can have on babies and their families.

Last winter our journey to start a family became reality. We were so excited to become first time parents. It had been 6 years since either side of our families had welcomed a baby. My dad was battling brain cancer and he wanted to become a grandpa again so badly. The timing was wonderful! We were elated but kept it quiet until the 'magic 12 week' mark. At 8 weeks I went to my first ultrasound. My husband decided to not come because he's a little squeamish about things and I myself didn't know what to expect. He'd have lots of other appointments to come to. I told him, "Don't worry about it, they won't tell us anything exciting, just an estimated due date, and we can kind of figure that out." Famous last words, it still makes me laugh. The ultrasound tech calmly said, "There's one, and there's two." WHAT?!?! 2??? No way, no how! No one on either side of our families has ever had twins. I thought that was the only way twins happened, besides IVF. The tech complimented me on how cool and collected it was. I explained that I didn't know her and didn't want to freak out in front of her, and that I thought I was still in shock. I went to the car and called my husband to tell him everything went well and that I'd tell him details when I got home. He happened to be grocery shopping, so I made sure he had picked up beer for himself! When I got home I showed him the ultrasound pictures, to which he replied, "Do they always call it Baby A?" We had separate pictures of them and then one together. We looked at each other in disbelief for quite a while, and over the next few days wrapped our brains around it. Was our spare room big enough for 2 cribs, would my mom still provide daycare if there are 2 of them, how are we going to fit all of their stuff into our cars...? The questions were soon followed by excitement and anticipation. We always wanted 2 kids, we were just getting them at the same time. It was a good deal for me, 1 bout of morning sickness, 1 delivery, one phase of lots and lots of poopy diapers. We could do this!

So on came the morning sickness, sciatica, bad head colds, and the stretching body! Out of the 21 weeks that I carried them I felt relatively good for only 2 or 3 weeks, but feeling like crud was a small price to pay for having 2 babies. At 12 weeks I saw a Perinatologist at our local hospital, only about 10 minutes from our house. I would go there for monthly ultrasounds as they confirmed at that appointment that they were definitely mono-di, like they had suspected from my first ultrasound. I thought like most people twins were either identical or fraternal. What did mono-di mean? We met with a Genetic counselor that day who discussed TTTS with us. What it is, what it looks like, the chances were of being affected by it, and what we could do about it.

We were in a good place, close to our hospital, seeing high-risk doctors, and close to Milwaukee, where one of the leading TTTS doctors practiced, and performed the surgery if we needed it. Things seemed to be going well for the most part, my morning sickness was starting to lessen, my belly was growing, and we were able to share our exciting news with people. At 16 weeks we found out we were having girls! At my 19-week appointment the fluid levels were starting to differ to a level that was concerning, I was put on immediate bed rest, while laying on my side and sipping my High Protein Boost. I was now scheduled for weekly ultrasounds, and was really scared. I knew this meant things weren't ok. I talked with Dr. DeLia from Milwaukee who worked closely with my peri. He seemed calm and collected and emailed me some resources. I knew what I had to do, so I followed his orders diligently. I am a kindergarten teacher and I was missing the last 2 weeks of school, which was emotionally difficult, put I kept my eyes on the prize! The following week at 20-weeks gestation, it looked like my hard work and determination had paid off. The fluid levels were balancing out a bit, bladders could be seen in both babies, dopplers were good, and their size was relatively similar. I went back home and continued with the same routine. However, this time it was tougher on my emotionally and physically. Emotionally I struggled because I knew I may have to do this for 3 more months, I was missing my favorite time of the school year, and I was unable to go visit my dad whose health was deteriorating. Physically, my hips hurt from laying on my side, my back was starting to hurt, I was having awful rib pain, and I was starting to get heartburn. But I kept my eyes on the prize.

I was excited to go to my 21-week appointment; to get up and take a shower, get out of the house, see my babies, and see why I was so uncomfortable. I had blown up like a balloon. The ultrasound took FOREVER! Baby A was struggling, no measurable fluid, no visible bladder, and stuck down really low. Baby B was swimming in a ton of fluid and they were starting to worry about her heart. My cervix changed as they measure it. I was scared to death. My doctor said I would need to have the laser surgery. I sobbed and sobbed. They took us into another room where we could talk. My doctor contacted Dr. DeLia in Milwaukee, where I'd go for surgery. He wanted an amnio reduction and cerclage done before I came to for the surgery. Without those 2 procedures, we would not make it to the surgery. I walked down the hallway to Labor and

Delivery. All I could think in my head was, "labor and delivery? I am NOT in labor and we are NOT delivering these babies, it's just a room where they are doing the amnio reduction." So that night the amnio reduction was done. Both babies looked good the whole time. As the procedure went on my rib pain started to go away; it was from all the extra fluid. They removed almost 3 liters of extra fluid! Gross! I was scheduled for a cerclage in the morning, and probably surgery in the next few days. I was having some cramping or contractions after the procedure, which I was told is normal because of the amount of fluid that was removed. The uterus needs to adjust. They gave me meds to stop the contractions, but they kept coming, getting more intense and more frequent. They gave me more meds, but nothing was working. Sometime in the middle of the night my water broke. It was Baby A's.

That's when I knew we were in real trouble. I knew the first 12 weeks of pregnancy were scary, and having twins at the end was scary. I knew full well that they would probably be in the NICU. I knew they may not come home at the same time, but I never let myself think that they would never come home. I never, ever thought we'd be in trouble at 21 weeks! My babies were coming. How do you prepare yourself for that? They were born that afternoon 9 minutes apart. Baby B,

Catherine, actually made her appearance first, followed by Baby A, Hattie. They were both born sleeping as labor was too tough on their tiny bodies. They were absolutely beautiful, just so teeny tiny. Catherine was 9 inches long and Hattie was 8.5 inches. They both weighed 10.5 ounces.

The nurses dressed them in adorable matching white dresses with pink hats and wrapped them up in blankets. They were baptized, held by both grandmas and one of their grandpas, and an aunt. We were able to keep them with us for 24 hours; the most rewarding, amazing, sad, and heart wrenching 24 hours of my life! 24 hours I will cherish forever! A few days later they were buried in the cemetery behind the church where we were married, next to my husband's grandparents.

Now what? I was frozen time. I couldn't do anything; I wasn't supposed to be doing anything. I was supposed to be pregnant, I was supposed to be on bed rest, I was supposed to be wearing maternity clothes. I was stuck. I cried harder than I ever knew I could cry; I cried more than I ever knew I could cry. What are you supposed to do? Where's the guide book? I believe I had a choice, I could stay right where I was, or I could move forward. (I hate the term move on, I'd never move on from this.) I made a goal for myself; Do one thing each day; go visit my dad, cook a meal, work on my baby book for angels, write a thank you; Just 1 thing. Put one foot in front of the other and see where it leads. Little by little I started to be able to do more.

At one point during that first month after losing the girls, I stumbled across a quote. "There is no foot so small that it cannot leave an imprint on this world." YES!!! That was it! That was my girls! I was madly in love with their amazing, little feet.

Their lives needed to mean something, they needed to be remembered.

Other people needed to know about TTTS! I drew inspiration from other TTTS angel moms that I had connected with on Facebook. Somehow, they had turned their grief into something powerful. They had taken something so sad and made it positive. As I lay in bed one night in tears, it came to me: The Catherine and Hattie Photo Challenge. I wanted people to say and write their names and talk about TTTS. Knowledge is power. The whole world needs to know about my girls and their courageous battle!

I stayed awake for hours thinking of how this could work. My tears turned into a smile. Man, did that smile feel good. I could remember my girls with a smile! I was on to something; something that could be big, something that could be powerful. The next morning I sat down on my computer and started typing. It poured out and my thoughts and the words came out perfectly. I posted the challenge to my two TTTS groups on Facebook. Within minutes people from all over the US had responded to the idea. Go little feet, go! Then people from other countries started to respond to the idea. Then I emailed friends and family who knew our story. Within a few days pictures started to come in. Each time I got one, I smiled a big smile (and maybe cried a few tears). My girls were telling the world about TTTS. How cool is that?

I was not at a place where I could share our story with all of my Facebook 'Friends'. I had also decided when I started the Photo Challenge that it would run for a year. For their 1st birthday, on June 8th, 2013. I will pull all of the photos together to put into a book in their memory. 6 months into it I have received around 200 photos from Italy, Australia, Japan, Puerto Rico, England, France, Canada, Hawaii, North Carolina, New York, Georgia, Las Vegas, Wisconsin, and many other places in the USA. Every time I get one I know that someone has thought about Cathcrinc and Hattie, and I can't describe what a great feeling that is! My girls and their battle with TTTS have changed the world, one picture at a time.

"No foot is so small that it cannot leave an imprint on the world" –

Matias and Mael

Shalina Johnson

The most beautiful image I have ever seen was our 8-week ultrasound. I will never forget the amazement and excitement I felt when the image appeared. I yelled "TWINS" before the tech could even get one word out. That's right, after a miscarriage 7 months prior, God heard my cry and blessed us double.

My obstetrician brought up concerns about Twin-to-Twin transfusion syndrome to my husband and I since our babies are identical and shared the same placenta. We were then sent to a fetal specialist who would also monitor my pregnancy.

I had such a wonderful smooth pregnancy and I loved everything about it. Later we found out we were having boys! We would soon be a family of six. Their two older brothers were very excited to add two more boys to our family. Our hearts were full.

At 18-weeks I went for a routine checkup, this day would change our lives forever. As the doctor was performing an ultrasound he noticed an extreme difference between their growth and with the heart of one of my babies. All of the joy and excitement we had was now replaced with fear and heartbreak.

After a sleepless night and many prayers, we made our way to the specialist the next morning. As the tech started the ultrasound she was very quiet and wide eyed. The doctor later came in to confirm that our boys did indeed have Twin-to-Twin transfusion syndrome. There are five stages of TTTS and my precious boys had already progressed to stage four. My recipient twin, who was receiving a majority of nutrition from the placenta, had overworked his body so much his heart was failing. His enlarged heart had minimal function, and opposite blood flow. He also had hydrops which is excess fluid around his heart, head and abdomen. While my donor twin, had minimal nutrition from the placenta, very little amniotic fluid in his sac which restricted movement, was anemic and 30% smaller than his brother.

I felt helpless and my mind couldn't even process the information I'm being told. In an instant my perfect pregnancy turned into my babies fight to survive. The doctor tells us I can get a laser procedure done to fuse the abnormally connected blood vessels that is causing the TTTS. Three hours later we were on a flight from Arizona to Colorado for the procedure.

We arrived to Children's Hospital Colorado that evening. Exhausted yet determined to fight for our twins. We were immediately taken in for an ultrasound and once again I had the privilege of seeing my beautiful boys.

The doctors gave us the rundown of how the procedure works, risks, complications, possible outcomes. Without this procedure, the fatality rate for my twins was 100%. We would do anything to save our boys and were prepared to have the procedure the next morning.

As I'm being wheeled into the cold and bright operating room, seeing a dozen medical staff waiting and staring back at me, all while classical music is being played, this felt like the beginning of a nightmare.

What was supposed to be an hour procedure turned into three hours. I woke as the doctors were stitching up my incisions. The first thing I asked was "Are my babies okay?". The anesthesiologist tells me "They are fine but we couldn't finish the procedure."

As the doctors started the procedure my uterus immediately starts to bleed into the recipient's sac. The amniotic fluid was no longer clear to see the placenta which they were to work on. They attempted to remove the foggy fluid and replace with clear fluid. This was unsuccessful and they could not move forward with the procedure. Then we're faced with two options. Option one was radiofrequency ablation. How could we take the life of one of our boys to possibly save the other? We couldn't. The second option was to do the procedure again the next day. Even though there were now more complications, the doctors agreed to try again. If this was unsuccessful there would be no other options.

Again, the next day I was wheeled back into operating room, same music, same faces, same nightmare. Three hours later I awoke to the news of a successful procedure. If anything negative were to happen to my babies it would be within 24 hours. The next day, now 19 weeks, the ultrasound had shown a stronger heartbeat in the recipient. Next, the most horrifying words were spoken to me " I'm sorry, we lost baby B." I remember wailing and kicking like a child. I was in absolute disbelief and shock. My husband kept saying " No, I won't believe that. This is not true". The doctors left us to have time alone and we sat in silence almost the entire night.

We stayed five more days until we were cleared to fly back home. Our survivors health was improving by the day. Two weeks passed and I noticed minimal movement from him. We went to the hospital and they monitored his heart and all seemed well. We were discharged to go home. Two days later, I felt no movement. We went to my fetal specialist that morning. Going in we had faith that all would be well. To our dismay, we were told that my precious baby had passed as I slept. My body felt warm, my heart was racing, tears were streaming down my face. I stared at my husband but had no words. There is no greater heart break than to hear your children have died.

We had a scheduled induction for the next morning, I was 21 weeks. After 13 hours of labor, I delivered my precious boys Matias and Mael Johnson. Born at 10:26pm and 10:28pm. Perfect hands, feet, eyebrows, just beautiful boys. They very much resembled their older brothers.

We will forever carry Matias and Mael in our hearts. We take comfort in knowing that one day we will meet them again.

Alana and Selena

Krystal Sierra

It was early October of 2010 when my boyfriend and I found out I was pregnant. We had so many different emotions that day. We had just moved to a new state and were staying with family until we were able to get on our feet. So finding out we were having a baby was a lot to put on us at that time, but of course the feelings of "what are we going to do" went away and on came the pure excitement. We told everyone in the family and they were all supportive. This being my first pregnancy I was very nervous but anxious at the same time.

In December is when we went in for our routine visit as my doctor was doing the ultrasound she told us there were two heart beats! I was then transferred to a different hospital because my doctor didn't handle high risk pregnancies and they consider any twins high risk.

That's where I met my new doctor, Dr. Guin. A couple weeks later we found out we were having two little girls!

I don't remember ever feeling as happy as I did the first time I felt my little girls move inside of me. They were a part of me and I couldn't wait to meet them. We'd talk about names and what they were going to look like. I felt so attached to my girls. I would rub my belly constantly as if I was already holding them in my arms. I remember going to the baby store and laughing with my boyfriend about how we were going to have to buy doubles of everything! How exciting, that I, out of all people, was going to be having twins! I never expected this and for some reason it felt like I was specially chosen to carry two lives.

My boyfriend and I went in to our routine ultrasound to see how our girls were doing and it went just like any other appointment. We were watching TV at home that evening and I received a call from Dr. Guin's partner. He explained to me that he reviewed my ultrasound and saw what might be the start of TTTS. He briefly explained that it was a disease that only identical twins get and it had nothing to do with me our my boyfriend. He told me it meant that basically one of my girls is transferring her oxygen and blood to the other. He asked us to come in the next day to meet with Dr. Guin. At that point I got a little upset, but my boyfriend calmed be down and told me to wait for what Dr. Guin was going to tell us.

The next day we went to our appointment and I was extremely nervous for what we were going to be told. She drew a picture to show us what was happening inside of me so it was easier for us to understand. We asked her a ton of questions and honestly, she wasn't very hopeful or very positive. She gave us all the statistics and gave us different options. One of those options was to terminate the pregnancy, which in my mind was never an option.

From that day on our pregnancy completely changed. We were doing ultrasounds twice a week, Mondays and Fridays. Dr. Guin referred me to a specialist in San Francisco as well as Seattle. I decided since I live in Portland that Seattle would be the best choice for us. We went there and all the doctors were very nice and informative. They also gave us a DVD with our ultra sound on it which I really appreciated. They ended up telling us we were not yet a candidate for surgery and to continue keeping a close eye on the girls.

It was January 24, 2011. We went in to our ultrasound appointment that morning. The ultrasound tech said she wanted Dr. Guin to join us to look at the babies. She came in and saw that their fluids were almost equal. Throughout our pregnancy she was very doubtful and basically told us no one makes it out alive with this disease. She began to tell us how she was wrong and she was very happy with what she was seeing. They joked about how we could relax now and pick names for our girls. Since Dr. Guin said they were doing so well she decided to cancel my Friday appointment and to have me come in that following Monday. We were very excited and happy with how that appointment went.

That weekend we went to an indoor car show and went on with our everyday lives. While we were there I constantly had to sit down and take breaks. I could feel my girls squirming around constantly, but I assumed they were just getting bigger so these feelings were normal.

The following Monday January 31, 2011 I returned to work and all day I felt a cramping that would come and go. I assumed it was growing pains since I had felt that earlier in my pregnancy. My boyfriend came and ate lunch with me and by then the cramps were more often and a little bit stronger. After lunch, I went back to work and decided to call my doctor. I was only able to talk to the nurse, she talked to Dr. Guin and suggested I leave work and lie down and drink lots of water. I followed her instructions and was home lying in bed for about 4 hours. By then the cramps were very often and extremely painful. I was home with my sister in law and my niece. I called the on-call doctor and he recommended I come in. So my sister in law drove me to the hospital. On the way there the pain was very intense; I didn't understand what was happening and why I was in so much pain.

We got to the hospital and I felt the nurses didn't realize how serious my condition was as they weren't attending to me as fast as they should have been, just coming in every now and then to say the doctor will be in soon. While waiting for the doctor, I was in excruciating pain. My sister-in-law became upset and ran out of the room to tell them we needed help.

Finally, they came in and examined me. The doctor told me she couldn't feel a cervix at all and that I was fully dilated. My heart sank and I asked her was there anything that we could do and sadly she told me no. We moved into a delivery room as my sister -in-law called our family as well as my boyfriend and told them all to rush over. Everything after that happened to fast. I couldn't wrap my head around what was happening. My boyfriend arrived as he saw me on the bed yelling out of pain. The doctor explained to him that the TTTS had picked up and I gained too much fliud which is causing me to go into labor. With a shocked face he said, "This is bad, huh?" The doctor looked at him and said, "Yes."

I told the nurse I felt them coming, and before I knew it I had given birth to both of my girls. They placed them in my arms as I stared at them and saw all my dreams fade away. The nurse told me they both had heartbeats. So, I held them until their heartbeats drifted away and they passed. By this time my family was all there taking turns holding the girls and saying their goodbyes. My boyfriend's family was on their way driving up from Reno. The nurses took pictures and made memory boxes for each of our girls. They told us we could have the girls all night with us if we wanted, but we decided to have them take them a couple hours after. I remember the nurses coming in, wrapping my daughters in two blankets and taking them away. Out of everything that had happened, that was probably the hardest part for me. I felt that they were really gone. I felt like my heart was being physically yanked on. I have never felt so much pain in my life. The next day my boyfriend's family arrived and they were very supportive and it was nice to see everyone come together when we were in need. I could leave the hospital that evening. They brought me downstairs in a wheelchair as I held the two memory boxes in my hands, and I broke down. I never imagined going through all of this and leaving the hospital with only boxes instead of my daughters. I felt mad, jealous, and sad. This wasn't how it was supposed to go.

Then we had to plan a funeral for our daughters. It was very small and short. We put them to rest and I felt so empty. One minute I had a belly with my two daughters kicking around and the next we were burying them. It wasn't right.

I am still grieving and I don't know if I'll ever be over what happened to us, my family. I miss and love them with every inch of my body. Saying I love them doesn't even express half of my feelings for Alana and Selena. I will always have a hole in my heart for them. They are now my angels and they will never be forgotten.

Heatherly Rose and Winter

Taylor, their mother

Taylor's experience shows how suddenly TTTS can occur and further emphasizes why earlier and more frequent ultrasounds are so important in multiples pregnancies.

Heatherly Rose Neveah and Winter Lille Jade

I found out March 3rd that I was pregnant. I went for my first appointment that month. They did an ultrasound that month. The ultrasound did not show twins. I went the next month they did a Doppler and my doctor or I suspected twins. I went back June 20th I found out I was having twins. My doctor was going to send me to UAMS. He told me I was having identical twin girls and that I had stage one of TTTS. They did not give me any advice on what to do. Or what I could do all they said was it was wait and see.

June 18th I went to my doctor. The technician told me that she did not like what she saw but I did not understand at the time what she meant. The nurse came in and told me that they did not see a heartbeat for either twin. I just start crying wanting Mychael there so badly but he had somewhere else he had to be at the same time as my appointment.

My doctor told me to go back to UAMS the next day since I had an appointment scheduled. I went back and they confirmed what my doctor had said. I was twenty weeks by this time.

That was Thursday.

I went to the hospital that Friday because I was hurting. The nurse hooked me up to a fetal monitor the monitor was picking up heartbeats so they hooked me up to another machine to be sure. The heartbeats that were heard were over a hundred and twenty mine was under a hundred. I went back to my doctor Monday and he told me the same thing that he told me last time and that UAMS told me... no heartbeats. I went home my best friend starts bawling in her husband's arms I was fine till she told him that I was the one that needed the hug and shoved me into his arms.

Then I broke down. She talked my doctor into inducing me closer to home. I went that Wednesday on

June 25th. My sister came down and stayed with me all day. She tried to talk my doctor into one more ultrasound to be sure but I was ready to get all of this behind me. Heatherly Rose Nevaeh was born at 10:29pm weighed 4oz and was 7inches. Winter Lillie Jade was born at 10:30pm weighed 8.3 oz. and was 8 ¾ inches.

Allanah and Liz

Liz Steuart

Allanah and Liz's Story

It was 4 months since we had lost our little boy Liam at 13 weeks when we found out we were pregnant again. I was excited but so scared as well. It wasn't until 8 weeks we found out we were having identical twins. I was in shock but I thought it was a miracle. I googled as much as I could on identical twins and was very concerned with all of the complications they could have because they shared a placenta.

I went for my 12-week scan with the Maternal Fetal Medicine Specialist and after over an hour of scanning I knew they were a little concerned. They said there was a bit of a size difference between the babies and Allanah (the bigger one) had a lot more fluid around her. This wasn't a shock to me because I had done a lot of reading about what this means. She said that it could be an early onset of Twin to Twin Transfusion syndrome or possibly Selected growth restriction. She said they would keep a close eye on me but there is nothing they can do until about 17 weeks when they can possible do surgery on the placenta to separate the blood vessels connecting the girls. They made another appointment for 2 weeks' time. It was the longest 2 weeks of my life but I was having twice a week scans with my GP so I knew they were still OK.

At 14-weeks, I was told that things had progressed and the fluid and size difference was getting bigger. At this stage, they couldn't measure the blood flow because they were too small. I was told to prepare for the worst that I might lose 1 or both even before my next checkup at 16 weeks. I burst into tears it wasn't the news we were hoping for and how do you prepare yourself for something like that.

At 16- weeks they still had strong heartbeats but the size difference between them now was about 30% and Liz had barley any fluid around her. The blood flow tests showed they were sharing blood vessels and Liz was pushing a lot of her blood to Allanah which is causing the extra fluid and possible heart failure. There was still nothing they could do at this gestation all we could do was pray for a miracle. They were fighters to have made it this far.

At 18-weeks I went in hoping for the best but expecting the worst. I knew they were still ok as I had had 4 scans with my GP but Liz also had not even 1 cm of fluid around her by this stage. I was hoping they could do surgery ASAP. Instead the doctor just said it was BAD. He didn't explain anything or give me any hope. I left distraught I wasn't ready to give up on my babies so why should he. I went to my GP and said I wanted a second opinion I needed some hope so she referred me to a private specialist. He managed to fit me in that day and after 3 hours with him he gave me some hope. He said as long as there was life there was hope but I would need the surgery within a week so to go to my next appointment at the hospital and see what they said. I was lucky enough to get a DVD of the hour ultrasound and a DVD with several 3D images. It was my birthday this day so this was the best birthday present ever to finally have some hope.

It was 19 weeks and 2specialists had scanned me for over an hour and a half. Finally, they said I needed surgery. They didn't want to wait too long and I booked in for surgery in 2 days' time. I was so scared I knew this was their last chance. I knew there were risks but I had to do it. I packed my bags the night before and got no sleep that night.

It was the 19th of July 2012 and I was being prepped for surgery. It took just over an hour and a half and I was told it went well they cut off 2 very big vessels and 5 smaller ones that were connecting the girls. It was going to be a few weeks though to see if it was successful. I was in a lot of pain and so tired. I had a lot of contractions afterwards which was normal and I was given medication to stop them. Two days later I was allowed to come home and go back in a few days to see how things were going. I had been home for 1 night and I started having contractions again. I didn't think too much of it but they didn't stop. I thought I better go to the hospital and get checked out I might need more medication to stop them. I had an internal done to check that my cervix wasn't dilating. There was a bit of blood and the doctor said it wasn't good but they would do a proper scan and have a good look. The doctor that did my surgery came and did the scan and internal ultrasounds to check my cervix. He told me it was long and closed so that was a good sign but wanted to admit me to give me medication to stop the contractions and keep an eye on me.

I had a lot of visitors throughout the day, the contractions weren't stopping but weren't getting any worse. My girls were kicking me and my family and friends could even feel them. That night about 6:30pm my husband and sister were there. My sister helped me to have a shower and the pain was horrible. The pressure was unbearable and I could hardly stand. I was now getting 4 contractions a minute. The midwife called a doctor and after another internal examination she told me I was 5 centimetres dilated and I needed to get to birth suites. I screamed, this couldn't be happening.

We got down to birth suites and I told myself i had to stay strong to try and get through the labour. I had never been in so much pain. (I laboured with me son for 20 hours before having any drugs) and this was so different. I was screaming and screaming and thought how am I going to do this. The girls were born at 9:42pm on the 22/7/12.

Allanah was alive and lived for 1 hour and 14 minutes and weighed 322 grams; Liz wasn't strong enough to make it through labour and only weighed 136 grams . We just held them and cried. I was shaking uncontrollably they midwife thought it was because of the drugs but my temperature was over 40 degrees. I then started bleeding a lot. I was soaking the bed every 10 minutes they thought they would have to take me to surgery. I had a very bad infection. I lost over a litre and a half of blood and wasn't well. I didn't care I just wanted my girls. Luckily the bleeding slowed and I didn't have to go to surgery. We spent 3 days in hospital and I was able to have my girls with me the whole time. We got hundreds of photos and lots of special cuddles. Saying goodbye was the hardest thing I have ever done.

We started organizing the funeral when we got home. We knew we wanted something private and we wanted the girls' ashes brought home. We have them now in a teddy bear a locket that I'll never take off. Unfortunately, 2 days after I was discharged my infection got worse and I was losing chunks of placenta. I ended up in surgery to remove what they had left in me. Going back to the hospital was so hard and this time my girls weren't with me.

I miss them so much and wish they were here but feel some peace knowing they are together. We have many photos around our house and have just finished their memory shelves. My little boy knows he has 2 little sisters that live in heaven.

Braxton and Connor

Bethany Gary

The room is dark and cold. As I lay flat on the examining table, I feel a sense of unease. Something is wrong and I can feel it. I can see it in their facial expressions, all of them. I turn to look into my mother's eyes and verify that she feels it too. She grabs my hand. The doctors aren't speaking. They are all just peering into the computer screen like they are searching for something. In this moment, seconds feel like minutes. I am consumed in my thoughts. Will I ever escape this agony of the uncertainty? What is going on? Why aren't the doctors speaking to me? Are they okay? As I am laying there, completely vulnerable and afraid, my heart picks up its speed. My palms begin to sweat in my mother's hands. Oh God, please let them be alright.

The doctor sits down and she motions for another

doctor to turn on the lights. After she cleans my stomach, I pull down my shirt over my pregnant belly and raise up to a sitting position. When I finally look into her eyes, she doesn't have to say a word because I already know. She speaks anyway. "Your babies have passed away." With these words, my life was forever changed.

I can't explain what happened next. All I remember is what I felt, and it was a lot. At first I was in shock. I remember thinking, Is this really happening to me? Am I having a bad dream? Will I wake up any second and this all just be a nightmare? The doctor spoke again and reality slapped me in the face. "You can deliver them today or in a few days, whichever would be best for you." Deliver them! I was just told I lost my twins and now I have to give birth to them! She went on to explain that they were 5 months' gestation so it had to be done. I had to experience my very first delivery of childbirth to twins whom weren't alive. I was to go through labor knowing that I could not take them home with me. I wasn't going to hear them cry as they came into the world. I was to give birth to two little boys and then bury them into the ground.

Once I processed everything into my mind, I became withdrawn. I withdrew from my doctors, my mother, even myself. It was like the life was just taken out of my soul. I completely shut down and stripped myself from any emotion. I don't remember the walk to the delivery room. I was a ghost walking the halls of a hospital. Not one tear escaped from my eyes because I didn't allow myself to feel. Looking back, I think it was my way of protecting my sanity. The pain was too much for me to deal with in that moment. So, I chose to suppress all of my emotions so that I could survive what was to come.

I don't remember much about being induced. I don't remember what was said among family or doctors in the delivery room as we waited. The pain medicine they gave me made me sleep most of the time. I faded in and out of consciousness. Everytime I woke was a nightmare. I wanted so sleep forever. I didn't want to deal with reality. I didn't want to face childbirth of stillborn twins who I had just named Braxton and Connor the week before.

The last time I woke, it was time to deliver. My mother was right by my side and holding my hand again. They were born within minutes. I didn't feel any physical pain because of the medicine. But the emotional pain started to slip right through that barrier I put up within myself and it was more painful than any physical pain I could ever endure. I did not hold them. I couldn't muster the courage to even look at them. It would have scarred me more than I am scarred now. I could not hold my lifeless babies who I gave birth to. Just knowing that I could not take them home with me was enough torture.

After they were taken from me, I began to feel hatred for myself. I began to feel, period. The agony flowed through my being. I wept for hours. The tears could not stop. I was filled with despair and hopelessness. The anguish of grief I felt sent me over the edge and I lost all my faith in God. My soul surrendered to waves of despair. I became numb. In other words, I felt dead.

Three days later we held a beautiful graveside funeral for my boys. After it was over I felt like everyone was moving on with their lives but for me they were all I could think about. I even dreamed of Braxton and Connor in my sleep. I went through a major depression. The medicine my doctor prescribed me didn't help so I quit taking them. Not many people know this but I attempted suicide. When I failed, all it took was one look in the mirror. I looked myself in the eyes and heard a voice saying "You are going to be okay." I believe that was God talking to me. From then on, I still struggled but I vowed to myself that I was going to brave every day in a positive manner.

Six months passed and I became pregnant again. I was so afraid the entire pregnancy. I didn't want to lose another child. I dreamed of horrible things that could be wrong with my child and had nightmares of delivering my baby under horrid circumstances. Anything and everything that could go wrong, I worried about. I was still a very sad person and cried almost every day I was carrying my baby.

On January 9, 2011 I gave birth to the most beautiful creature I had ever seen. From the moment I heard her cry for the first time I fell in love. When she was placed in my arms I wept happy tears and could not take my eyes off her. As far as I was concerned, she and I were the only ones present in the world. Just her and I, with me locked in a wondrous gaze down at my little miracle. I named her Mallory, and she saved my life. She brought back all my hopes, dreams, and faith. Once again, I heard that voice, "You are going to be okay."

Nine months later I became pregnant once more with another baby girl. Those same fears had returned. The doctors reassured me that she was fine the entire pregnancy, however I still had my doubts. I didn't want to get my hopes up. I just couldn't afford to. Unless you've experienced the loss of a child, it would be difficult to understand the pain.

On March 11, 2012 MaKaya was born. As soon as I got to hold her, she peed on my arm. It made me laugh and cry, because I knew she was okay. After she was bathed we got to feed her. But something terrible happened. She got red in the face and couldn't breathe. She was rushed to the nursery as I lay there helpless. I couldn't move because of the effects of the epidural. I started to panic. The nurse calmed me down by reassuring me she was still alive and okay. She had a bowel loop in her intestine and had to stay in the nursery for 24 hours. Words cannot express how much I longed to have my baby with me. Once I got her back, I was so happy.

I now have two beautiful daughters with so much spunk and personality. They are funny, smart, and so sweet. I know I am truly blessed to be a mother. From time to time, I still am reminded of my twin boys. I imagine how old they would be, what they would look like and how they would act. It makes me sad to think of those things. I still struggle with depression to this day. I try my best not to let my children see me when I cry. I don't want them to see me as a sad person. I want to be strong for them. But even I have my weak days.

I know that everything happens for a reason. I believe I lost the twins because God wanted me to grow and learn from it. I am a different person now than I was then. I believe I have a greater appreciation for life and everything that happens. One of my life mottos is "Search for the rainbow after every storm." What this means to me is that I should look for the silver lining in every bad situation I am thrown into. There is always a positive, you just have to believe in it and search for it. Life is a beautiful, magical thing. The saying, "Don't forget to stop and smell the roses" is about the best advice anyone could ever give. It's the little things in life that mean the most. Sometimes we get so busy with everyday life that we start taking things and loved ones for granted. We need to remember that our lives are a special gift. We need to stop worrying about growing old, because that is a privelege denied to many! The last thing I want to say to anyone reading this; live well, love much, and laugh often.

Forever Linked

Erin Bruch

Growing up, I used to think that my life would have been a story. I thought there would be a beginning, middle, and an end. I'd grow up, go to college, get married, buy a house, and have a family.

Since I tried to fend off Twin to Twin Transfusion Syndrome (TTTS), my life completely changed. I wrote a book; *Forever Linked, A Mothers Journey through Twin to Twin Transfusion Syndrome*, published in 2011 less than 3 years after my sons died to TTTS.

But it seems a harder task to live today then to simply publish a book designed to explain the disease and explain how and why women and families made the medical decisions they did. I worked full time as a kitchen designer, took care of my eldest, and became pregnant with our last child during my writing process. I spoke to doctors on every continent, except Antarctica, and South America. I would work my day job, come home, cook and clean, take to play with my daughter, spend some time talking with my husband, then switch gears and begin writing from 11 PM to 1 AM. I'd get up the next day, and do it again, because I wanted to help moms. I felt that moms who are facing this disease needed a trusted easy to understand explanation of the disease. I did that. I got every treatment option with multiple outcomes to aid families to understand that a newly diagnosed mom is thinking and feeling.

I guess my personal goal of *Forever Linked* was to explain and show that in the moment every family will make a different decision and that is fine. But that each family is also at the mercy of a disease we can't physically look at.

The reality is this disease is just scary. Even if you have the laser surgery, your children are not safe.

My life now will have two stories; one living before TTTS, the other after. I still wake up with the same pain of the loss, I know my family misses them. I can remember the day of the funeral in pieces; I'll never fully remember it all. I know I will continue having PTSD due to my own TTTS experience.

See, I live knowing that my sons make others feel uncomfortable, which when I say that sentence to myself it pisses me off. I hear every day, "Maybe if you would have prayed more, God would have let you have them." or "God gave you this cross to carry.". I was so lost at first, my religious friends infuriated me. It wasn't until, I a Roman Catholic woman, walked into a Jewish Synagogue. The Rabi explained how his family and friends had been torn apart by WWII. But what amazed me the most was him saying "My god didn't pick and choose who lived and who died by the Nazi's hands. Why would I follow a god that treats his people so?" He's was right, I do not carry a cross, I just endured a hard part of life, but I am still alive.

For everyone who asks. "Erin, who has the worst or saddest story in *Forever Linked*?" My reply now is, "Why do you want to judge and grade these moms' terror? No one's lost or experience is more or less painful." What we need to do now, is help each other through it. We should not judge each other.

I am still trying to get my feet underneath me, which seems odd because it's been 7 years now. I am trying to forgive my body for TTTS. I say to myself everyday now, "I forgive my body for creating TTTS." It was the egg that split at that certain time that caused the condition Twin to Twin Transfusion Syndrome. It is a disease that nature randomly makes and cannot be prevented. Once I have overcome that, I need to forgive myself for the decisions I made. Since the deaths, I had leaned by a pathology report done on my son's placenta. That had we selected the "Sicker" twin, the other would have survived. They had a 50/50 split on the placenta; he had enough room to survive the remainder of the pregnancy. I understand that a mom must be able to make the medical decision regarding her body. No one should ever judge her for it, but they can help her through her decision. I do regret not saving Vincent. And I watched both of my sons die because I failed to act. As you can tell, I still have issues I need to face.

I will continue to work on me, on my own personal reflection. While parenting our living children, we (my husband and I) pray every night and remember the boys as the therapist suggested. We went to a family therapist after the boys passed. The therapist said death is a part of life and the loss of the boys should be a part of life for them. The concept seemed correct and made sense.

To this day, I do try and stay in touch with other TTTS mom's and familie. I try and help a group of moms who send out care packages to families who have endured a loss : the TTTS SUPPORT TEAM. I love that organization; having something physical can give a family who lost a child a sense of normalcy which is medicine in its own right.

Part 4
Giving Back

Here to Help

So many parents who have experienced TTTS, the loss of a child, prematurity, or any combination, take the energy from this experience into trying to make the world a better place for those who will follow them.

This chapter just talks about a few of them. The TTTS Support Team, Sunshine After the Storm, the TTTS Walk for Life, and Teeny Tears.

TTTS Support Team

I remember when I saw the Facebook post from Christina. It read:

"The T.T.T.S Support Team was created in 2011 by a group of parents who have been affected by T.T.T.S. We remember the intense pain and worry we felt as we dealt with this disease and we would like to help other women who are finding themselves in this dark place.

If you or someone you know is suffering a loss from Twin To Twin Transfusion Syndrome we would like to send you a care package. The package includes a grief pamphlet, a list of helpful resources, and some fun surprises to bring a smile to your face during these hard days. The packages are completely free of charge and 100% donated by another T.T.T.S parent. They are available to everyone regardless of your location.

If you would like to be sent a care package from another T.T.T.S parent, please message your name, mailing address, and your story via Facebook or email."

I immediately sent an email to Christina and shared my story.

She matched me with someone in my area.

When I received my package from Rachel. I was blown away by her thoughtfulness and the items that she put into the package. She sent me a note and told me that she had also lost one of her twins to TTTS. And, turns out, she lives in the same city. The package included a frame for Kathryn, a journal, some comfy socks, support materials, and other items meant to pamper and comfort me.

We were immediately bonded.

The package changed my life. That seems a little over dramatic, but it's a true statement. One, I realized there were others in my city who had experienced this dreadful nightmare. We began to find each other and form a local support group.

Two - I realized I really wanted to give back too.

I asked Christina how I could be a part of the team.

She said all I had to do was volunteer and be willing to be matched and send packages.

And so it began.

As mentioned above, the TTTS Support Team is 100% volunteer. You ask to join the team, and then are matched with mothers who have lost one or both twins. We take full responsibility for putting together and sending packages. There are some items that were donated in bulk that Christina sends out as she has the money, but for the most part, we pay completely out of pocket.

And that gets expensive.

Christina and her crew have now formed a nonprofit and collect donations so that they can purchase items to send to the team to bring down the costs for volunteers.

It warms my heart to know I might bring a moment of happiness to a mother during this time of mourning.

Find out more at http://www.tttsgriefsupport.com/

Sunshine After the Storm

In October 2013, I edited and self published my first book, Sunshine After the Storm: A Survival Guide for the Grieving Mother. I rounded up over thirty other parents who had experienced the loss of a pregnancy, infant, or child, or have had to deal with infertility. While I wrote the frame of the book, the heart and soul comes from the individual stories that are shared within.

We share our personal experiences with loss, but also how we survived it. And what you, if you are a grieving mother, or someone supporting a grieving mother, can do to survive.

We cover a broad gamut of topics, from multiple pregnancies losses, to stillbirth, infant loss, to the loss of older children. We share stories of infertility, and stories of wavering faith. We cover horrible, and good things that were done for us and said to us. We talk about how fathers grieve differently and the difficulties a relationship can face after the loss. We talk about the good that has come from our losses, such as the creation of the TTTS Support Team, Teeny Tears, Finding My Muchness, Donna Day (Donna's Good Things), Molly Bears, Naomi's Circle, Mikayla's Grace, A

Little Thunder, the film about stillbirth Return to Zero, and so many other wonderful support organizations that have been formed because of the impact a loss of a child had on someone.

Writing this book was so cathartic for all of us. We wanted to get it out to as many grieving parents as we could. So we gave free copies of the ebook for several days. More than 1700 copies were downloaded. We began to receive amazing feedback and we realized what a positive impact this book of hope and encouragement could be.

Not long after I decided to take it to the next level. I created Sunshine After the Storm, Inc., a nonprofit with the goal of raising funds to cover the costs of donating the book free of charge to NICUs, bereavement support groups, churches, and the like. We also send care packages to grieving mothers. We have now donated over 200 copies of the book.

Find out more at http://sunshineafterstorm.us

TTTS Walk for Life

The Walker and Willis TTTS Walk for Life

Brooke Myrick and family host the annual Walker and Willis Birthday Walk for Life.

After attending a walk sponsored by the TTTS

Foundation in Ohio, Walker, whose twin passed away in utero, asked his mother Brooke if they could sponsor a birthday walk in honor of his twin Willis. It would raise money for the TTTS Foundation.

Brooke and Walker are especially interested in promoting this walk to raise more awareness for the community about TTTS. Early detection is such a key factor in saving both twins suffering from TTTS, but mothers have to know to ask questions of their doctors because even today, many OBs do not take TTTS as seriously as they should. In Brooke's case, similar to mine, she went four weeks between ultra sounds. By the time the TTTS was detected, it was too late.

This loss greatly impacted them. Brooke and her family have been extremely open about talking about Willis, TTTS, and raising awareness to help future mothers of twins.

Brooke learned about the Ohio TTTS walk through a support group, she said, and support groups have been instrumental for Brooke in dealing with the loss of her son.

Teeny Tears Founded by Megan Branham

As we came closer and closer to Dex and Crew's third birthday, I began searching for a project that would honor Dex's memory and give purpose to my grief. I was looking for something economical, meaningful, and within my limited sewing abilities.

I would make tiny little diapers for stillborn micro preemie infants and those that pass away in the NICU. We launched Teeny Tears.

Approximately 26,000 children are stillborn in the United States every year, about 1 in 160 births. Another 19,000 children die within the first 28 days of life. A significant number of these angels are preemie or micro preemie infants. The littlest angels are so small that even the very tiniest Pampers NICU diaper is far too large for them. Besides that, their skin is so delicate that commercial diapers are very damaging.

Our volunteers donate to hospitals and bereavement support organizations at no charge. These small diapers fit angels between 18 and 23 weeks gestation. The large ones fit angels between about 24 and 30 or 32 weeks. The need for these diapers is enormous and endless. Gone are the days when angel babies must be left with naked bums because there is nothing suitable. No longer must nurses try to fashion a "diaper" out of cotton balls and tape. Our little diapers offer dignity and modesty to the tiniest angel babies. We provide two diapers per family, so that the parents don't have to choose whether to keep the diaper in a memory box or to bury the diaper with their child. This way they can do both.

Grieving parents often feel very lost, alone, and confused. Every special effort to honor their loss goes a long way. It is very difficult for a family to say goodbye to their child before they got to say a decent hello. These diapers, made with love, tell parents that someone understands that their child existed, that they are special, loved, real, and that they matter. The love that goes into these diapers tells a grieving parent that someone understands that their loss is tremendous. Because "a person's a person, no matter how small."

As you can imagine, November is always a tender time of year for our family. The year we launched Teeny Tears was the first November that I didn't spend the first half of the month hiding under my covers in bed, eating chocolate leftover from Halloween. As I sewed for angel families, I felt close to my son and my heart was filled with love and a peace I didn't know was possible.

Teeny Tears is my way to make sure that Dex and all of his angel friends are remembered. It has been an unexpectedly joyful and healing endeavor and I have met some of the most caring and generous people along the way. Many of our volunteers are angel families themselves, some of them still the walking wounded. As they participate in serving others in a similar plight, a miracle happens. They find their own sorrows lessened and their hearts begin to heal. Joy is found and lives are changed.

As an inexpensive, simple, unique, educational, and meaningful service opportunity, families are sewing our diapers, sewing clubs, youth groups, Eagle Projects, Angel Mother grief support organizations, and churches of all religious denominations. We encourage our volunteers to donate within their local communities and we also match volunteers with hospitals all over the country on our growing waiting list. Grandmothers are digging their flannel scraps out of storage, families are repurposing old receiving blankets and shopping yard sales for fabric remnants. And we know when all the fabric sales are going on!

To date, our volunteers have donated more than 180,000 diapers to grieving angel families across the world. While I wish no one ever needed our diapers, I am pleased that there is something that we can try to do for these families to let them know that they are not alone.

Find out more at http://teenytears.blogspot.com/

Part 5

How to Support a Grieving Parent

NEVER THE SAME

Supporting Grieving Parents

Sadly, I know far too much about being a mother who has lost a baby. In the time since Kathryn died, I have spent a large amount of time with other mothers who have lost a baby or child.

I can tell you one thing with certainty – no two people are the same, women all grieve differently, and I can give you all the advice in the world that has worked for me and others I know, but you have to choose the suggestions that are most appropriate for your friend or loved one and their personality.

But, the other thing I also know is that no matter what, don't be afraid to say or do SOMETHING. The worst mistake is avoiding and ignoring. Many mothers see this as hurtful, because they feel it doesn't matter to you. So, let them know you care and love them, and while you are struggling to know what to do or say, you are always there to listen if they want to talk.

Watching a friend suffer the loss of a child or baby is

one of the most difficult situations you may ever encounter in life. Surviving infant loss is one of the worst experiences a mother can go through. Loss and death combined with what is typically a positive, joyous occasion puts a mother into a state of shock and despair, while their friends struggle to know what to do and say.

There are few words, and even the words you do find never seem to be enough or appropriate. This type of unexpected grief can be extremely isolating to the mother who has experienced the loss of a baby, exacerbated by friends and family who often do not know how to respond or react. You may want to read my tips on things to say or not to say after someone loses a baby. More than anything, be sensitive!

The first year after infant loss is especially difficult. The unexpected nature of the loss brings pain, and the pain becomes fresh again as she passes through all of the "markers" and baby anniversaries, the dreaded "year of firsts." Rather than feel helpless when a friend or family member loses a child and saying and doing nothing in response, here are some actions you can take to support your friend or loved one through their loss.

I've got some ideas and suggestions that can help you in this journey. And thank you, for caring enough about her to try.

Months 1-3

Visit often, but not too often. Even if she says she does not want visitors, show up anyway, even if to just drop off some food or a gift of encouragement. I thought I wanted to be alone in my grief after I lost my baby when she was only two days old, but was always relieved when I received visitors. Ignore protestations at least until you can assess how welcome you are, yourself.

Take meals. More than once. There are many days that will be overwhelming throughout the first few months and even perhaps into the second year. You can use sites such as Care Calendar, which is an easy to access, online calendar to coordinate with other friends and families to provide meals. Those who want to help can sign up online for the day they will bring a meal or visit to help spread it out.

Talk about it with her! Don't pretend like nothing happened. Be sure to ask what she is comfortable talking about. Some loss mothers prefer not to talk about it, yet others find such healing and comfort in saying their baby's name. This baby is significant to the mother, and it is important to the mother that others recognize and remember the baby too. Even if only pregnant for a short time, mothers bond with their babies, and appreciate being recognized as a mother to that child. Read up on appropriate things to say or not to say after a loss of this nature. If all else fails, just let her know you are sorry for her loss and you are listening.

Make her laugh. For me, this was important, but guage this on the personality of the person. Some people don't want to laugh, and that's okay too. Everyone processes grief differently. In my case, laughter was a saving grace. Several days after my two-day-old daughter died, my sister and a friend came to visit one evening. My friend Debbie is a hoot. She had me laughing so hard and it felt really great. I really needed that. If you are not very comedic yourself, perhaps bring over a hilarious movie or find some funny YouTube clips.

Offer to help put away baby items. This is an extremely difficult task for a mother grieving the loss of her baby. You can volunteer to pack up clothing, toys, or nursery items and remove them for her if your friend is not up to handling this chore. Or volunteer to help her if she needs some support while she is doing this task.

Months 4-6

Continue some or all of the above and also:

Help with childcare. If your friend has other children, take them for an afternoon, evening, weekend, or whatever you can handle.

Send cards randomly. Not just once, but periodically. Especially around any significant dates that could trigger sadness like the due date, the anniversary of the death, or the date when a diagnosis was received. Just when you think "she should be over it," send another card. It's quite possible, she will never be over her loss.

Take her out. Any place. And if she says no to your invitations, keep inviting her. Eventually she will be ready.

Show her you also remember the baby. Bring trinkets with the baby's name on it if she appreciates them. If you are unsure, make donations in the baby's name to appropriate foundations. (Be sure to ask the parents if they have a preferred philanthropy.)

Encourage her to find a baby loss support group. I am part of a local loss group focused on parenting after loss. It is so cathartic for me to be surrounded by other mothers who have experienced the loss but are still raising other small children. While you can listen to her all day, if you have never experienced this type of loss, it's difficult to understand. Your friend will benefit from being around mothers who "get her."

Months 6-12

Continue some or all of the above and also:

Help her get involved in Pregnancy and Infant Awareness Day. October 15th is International Pregnancy and Infant Loss Awareness Day. Most major metropolitan areas have events planned, such as walks to remember. Visit October 15th to find out more.

Be patient. Those who have never experienced a loss may find it very difficult to understand how a mother can grieve and mourn for so long. But this loss stays with a mother for a lifetime. She is not angling for attention. She is hurting. And sometimes year two is even more difficult.

Please remember the average heaviest grieving period is 18-24 months.

If you attempt even a fraction of these steps, you are an outstanding friend and will make a big difference in supporting the grieving process of your friend. Of course, you can't take your friend's pain away. But you can do the next best thing: you can be there for her while she goes through it and hopefully ease her burden with your sturdy, non-judgmental presence.

When visiting and speaking to your friend, here are some things I think you should avoid saying:

1. "It's all part of God's plan." Many people may believe this to be true, but not what I wanted to hear after losing my baby. And the idea that God would target people to lose babies or to go through the kind of Hell our family went through is just absurd to me.

2. "You can have another one." Thankfully, no one said this to me, but I've heard several women say they heard this. Very VERY inappropriate!

3. "Everything happens for a reason." Not what I wanted to hear. I did not... COULD NOT... understand why it happened and certainly was not in a place to think through the possible reasons behind it or what good may one day come from it.

4. "God only gives us what we can handle." Nope. I'm not buying it. I'm pretty sure I went well past my threshold, but was thankfully saved by loving family and friends and my other three children. Now I will believe that God provided me with that support network, however, immediately after losing my baby I did not find this statement reassuring.

5. "The baby is in a better place." Most mother's

think the best place for their newborn is in their loving arms. Although the sentiment behind this statement is understood, it's best to just not say it.

Resources for the Grieving Mother

Online Resources and Support

Sunshine After the Storm - Support for Grieving Parents **and** Sunshine After the Storm: A Survival Guide for the Grieving Mother **(book)**

October 15th website

First Candle

Glow in the Woods

Still Standing Magazine

CarlyMarie - Project Heal and The Seashore of Remembrance

Still Breathing

The Rainbow Collection

Finding My Muchness

Sherokee Ilse, Author

Teske Drake, Author

Nora's Nook and Gifts

Thank You

This book would not have been possible without all of the input from the many families who shared their stories. Thank you for trusting me with your words, your journeys, and your precious babies' stories. Every time we share our stories, the world gets safer for future TTTS babies. Thank you also for your friendship.

Thank you especially to my family, for putting up with me spending long hours at the computer.

Thank you most of all to Charis, for being such a fighter and survivor, when the odds were certainly not in her favor.

About the Author

Alexa Bigwarfe is a wife, mother of three, author, freelance writer, and blogger. She is an avid advocate for those without a voice of their own. She started blogging as an outlet for her grief after the loss of one of her twin daughters to Twin to Twin Transfusion Syndrome (TTTS). She is co-author of the book *Lose the Cape: Realities from Busy Modern Moms and Strategies to Survive.* She also edited and published a book for grieving mothers entitled *Sunshine After the Storm: A Survival Guide for the Grieving Mother.* You can find out more about Alexa on her blog http://katbiggie.com or her professional website http://writepublishsell.co.

www.ingramcontent.com/pod-product-compliance
Lightning Source LLC
Chambersburg PA
CBHW050622300426
44112CB00012B/1622